ADVENTURES IN COMPLEXITY

For organisations near the edge of chaos

LESLEY KUHN

Published in this first edition in 2009 by:
Triarchy Press
Station Offices
Axminster
Devon. EX13 5PF
United Kingdom

+44 (0)1297 631456
info@triarchypress.com
www.triarchypress.com

© Lesley Kuhn 2009.

The right of Lesley Kuhn to be identified as the author of this book has been asserted by her in accordance with the Copyright, Designs and Patents Act, 1988.

All rights reserved.

No part of this publication may be reproduced, stored in a retrieval system or transmitted in any form or by any means including photocopying, electronic, mechanical, recording or otherwise, without the prior written permission of the publisher.

A catalogue record for this book is available from the British Library.

Cover design and image by Heather Fallows.
www.whitespacegallery.org.uk

ISBN: 978-0-9562631-0-0

Triarchy Press Ltd.

Contents

PREFACE		vii
1. INTRODUCTION		
1.1	Setting the scene	1
1.2	Being near the edge of chaos	4
1.3	From seeing through a lens to seeing the lens	6
1.4	How what goes around changes what comes around	8
1.5	What can a complexity view offer?	11
1.6	The shape of this book	14
2. ORGANISATIONS AND COMPLEXITY		
2.1	Fractal fragment (1) Jay and Bilal, Outreach Loans Bank	17
2.2	Introducing a complexity paradigm	19
2.3	Organising or arranging: what's the difference?	21
2.4	A complexity cosmography	24
	2.4.1 Self-organisation	26
	2.4.2 Dynamism	29
	2.4.3 Emergence	31
2.5	Modern management theory and complexity	37
2.6	A complexity analysis of fractal fragment (1) Outreach Loans Bank	38
	2.6.1 Introducing the complexity metaphor fitness landscape	39
3. COMPLEXITY PHRASE SPACE		
3.1	Metaphors and concepts in sense making	44
3.2	Fractal fragment (3) Ryan, Liverpool Catholic Club	45
3.3	Complexity metaphors	47
	3.3.1 Phase space – phrase space	48
	3.3.2 Communicative connectedness	52
	3.3.3 Sensitive dependence on initial conditions	56

		3.3.4	Edge of chaos – chaotic edge	59
		3.3.5	Attractors	60
		3.3.6	Fractality	63
	3.4	Fractal fragment (4) Hanna, Lifeguard International Insurance Company		71
	3.5	A complexity analysis of fractal fragment (4)		75
	3.6	From complexity-based analysis to complexity-inspired ways of organising		79

4. IDENTIFYING PATTERNS AND POTENTIALITY

	4.1	Complexity-based pattern analysis		83
	4.2	Complexity-based inquiry methods		85
		4.2.1	Coherent conversations	86
		4.2.2	Fractal analysis	87
		4.2.3	Attractor analysis	88
		4.2.4	Useful questions for complexity-informed inquirers	88
	4.3	Enhancing knowledge management at Multi-national Pharmaceuticals: fractal fragment (5)		89
	4.4.	Fractal fragment (6) Phil, The KIA Group		100
	4.5	Identification of pattern and potentiality in fractal fragment (7) Australian Stuttering Research Centre		104
	4.6	A very useful attractor set		108
	4.7	Complexity, self-organisation and ethical management		112

5. ORGANISING AT THE EDGE OF CHAOS

	5.1	Competencies commensurate with organising at the edge of chaos	119
	5.2	What can an organisation do to enhance its opportunities in a complex world?	120

REFERENCES	126
About the Author	129
Testimonials	130

List of Figures

Figure 1	Separation and interconnection between organisations and perspectives (ideas about organisations)	7
Figure 2	Examples of the dialectical and reciprocal process of evolving thought and action	10
Figure 3	Fractality depicted in the repeated branching of a fern	65
Figure 4	Fractality depicted in Stephen Wolfram's computer simulation of repeated triangles	65
Figure 5	The Great Wave by Katsushika Hokusai (1760-1849)	66
Figure 6	The Deluge by Leonardo Da Vinci (1452-1519)	67
Figure 7	Universal Human Attractor Set	108

List of Fractal Fragments

Fractal Fragment 1	Outreach Loans Bank Jay and Bilal	Chapter 2
Fractal fragment 2	Liverpool Catholic Club Ryan	Chapter 3
Fractal fragment 3	Lifeguard International Insurance Company Hanna	Chapter 3
Fractal fragment 4	National Counselling Service Anna	Chapter 1 Chapter 4
Fractal fragment 5	Enhancing knowledge management Multi-national Pharmaceuticals	Chapter 4
Fractal fragment 6	Kiwis in Australia (KIA) Phil	Chapter 4
Fractal fragment 7	Australian Stuttering Research Centre Mark	Chapter 1 Chapter 4

PREFACE

This book is intended for people who are concerned with improving organisational processes and practices. It is written for people who work for, in, or with organisations, and people who own, direct or have responsibility for managing organisations. In writing this book I seek a balance between being overly theoretical, and therefore at risk of boring those with whom I most want to communicate, and writing in a superficially popular, faddish style, which to my mind is grossly disrespectful of practitioners. I want to achieve a balance between theorising and exploring experiences.

I come from a transdisciplinary background that transverses education and learning, music, human geography, environmental science, organisation studies, psychology and philosophy, to name probably the most dominant areas of experience, and I have been delighted to find in the complexity sciences principles that are applicable and useful across all of these disciplines. Engaging with the ideas and language of what my colleagues and I at first referred to as chaos theory and what we now describe as the complexity sciences, I have found a rich source of models and images that have helped me to make breakthroughs in my understanding of and ways of engaging with these disciplines and beyond.

My experiences in organisations constantly remind me of complexity principles. Over time this has inspired me to work with these principles in organisational settings – where I am continuously refining and developing my thinking (theorising). Some of my writing here is a reflection of this cycle.

Two overriding assumptions guide me in introducing a complexity approach to organising and studying organisations. The first is that, at a most basic level, it seems human life is totally bound up with collectives of various kinds. Reflecting on organisations and processes of organising, therefore, inescapably requires us to ask fundamental questions about what it means to be human and about the nature of human society. My second assumption is that we are all theorists of one kind or another. We tell others and ourselves stories about what has happened, what will happen and why. Unfortunately, many of us have learned to accept other's theories as our own, and find ourselves repeating explanations of what are just the dominant ideas of the collectives of our experience.

In my introduction to a complexity theoretical perspective I will, therefore, take readers into a little philosophical reflection and present a challenge to dominant organisation theories and the assumed correctness of many familiar practices. While some may think of theory as cold or irrelevant, theory in my experience guides everyday practices. In theorising I am attempting to bring some sophistication of thought to what, at times, have become routine and repetitive processes. For me, theorising is exploration. Often this exploration creates the

PREFACE

potential for generating useful and productive insights. At times theorising is an intellectually rewarding activity, and it is in this frame of mind that I am reminded of D. H. Lawrence's poem 'Thought' (Sagar, 1972):

Thought, I love thought.
But not the jiggling and twisting of already existent ideas
I despise that self-important game.
Thought is the welling up of unknown life into consciousness,
Thought is the testing of statements on the touchstone of the conscience,
Thought is gazing on to the face of life, and reading what can be read,
Thought is pondering over experience, and coming to a conclusion.
Thought is not a trick, or an exercise, or a set of dodges,
Thought is a man in his wholeness wholly attending.

Thoughtfulness matters in a society dominated by organisational life. Most people work for large organisations for many of their waking hours. Employment in organisations where the leaders or management demand certain responses, and where in order to stay 'safe' employees must respond accordingly, has implications for the sorts of habits of thought that develop. The habits of thought give shape to the kinds of society we inhabit. We need to separate learning to be wise (thoughtful) from learning to be wily (surviving in an organisational setting), for without this the future of civil society is in jeopardy.

This book would not have made it to publication without the assistance of a great many people. It was a collective act of kindness and generosity of spirit that allowed me to engage with the thoughts and concepts that have led to this book. I write because we are.

Lesley Kuhn, 2008

References

Sagar, K. (1972) *D. H. Lawrence Selected Poems.* Middlesex: Penguin Books.

1. INTRODUCTION

1.1 Setting the scene

This book seeks to bridge the divide between work practices and the growing body of complexity-based organisation literature. My intention is to demonstrate, in an accessible manner, how complexity habits of thought, metaphors and concepts can be used to create new understandings and approaches to organisational structure, processes, issues and practices.

Organising to 'get things done' presents a number of organisational challenges. In recent interviews where I asked people about how, and how well, their organisations organise, I was given a wide variety of answers. Mark and Anna, quoted below, describe two very different approaches.

We get things done by sheer, creative, driving excitement and people who can do it. In general we are devoid of any known management structure in the universe. We don't say things like "they're not problems, they're challenges". We don't have lines of authority; we don't do change management. It's organised chaos....
Professor Mark Onslow, Australian Stuttering Research Centre.

Our organisation is very hierarchical. I'm answerable to my boss, and he's answerable to his, and his boss is answerable to the board. So the way we get things done, is by this hierarchical chain. It means poor communication and poor information dissemination. If I have concerns and want decisions made, I discuss these with my boss at our monthly meetings. I then have to wait for him to take the matter to his boss, who then takes it to the board. Everything takes a long time because we are so hierarchical.
Anna, National Counselling Service, Australia.

These ways of organising do not arise out of nowhere. Each approach has been influenced by past histories. The people involved in each organisation bring their assumptions, ideas and preferences. Organisational

1. INTRODUCTION

practices thus have very long and tangled trailing histories, implicating a great many personal experiences and theoretical frameworks about how best to 'get things done' in an organisation.

In this book, complexity habits of thought and metaphors are introduced and used to provide original and thought provoking ways of understanding organisational forms, processes and practices. Assuming that new ways of seeing lead to new strategies of action, a complexity approach is used to effectively reinterpret organisation-related issues and problems that have long remained irritating and difficult for theoreticians and practitioners alike.

The complexity approach that I outline brings together recent developments in areas such as neurobiology, psychology, philosophy, sociology and anthropology. Complexity and its range of applications are explored through:

1. taking major organisational concepts and exploring these from a complexity perspective and
2. presenting case studies of contemporary organisational experiences and demonstrating complexity analytical methods for making sense of these.

Over recent years I have been drawn to complexity theory or science as a way of understanding social phenomena. In this book I wish to unfold this theory for improving how we make sense of and explain organisational life. Doing this presents a challenge: I have to say enough about a complexity approach for you to see its relevance, but without the detail that would require knowledge of specialised complexity language. To manage this difficulty I use stories, garnered from recent interviews, as a starting point for explaining specific complexity concepts and to show how complexity can help identify organisational processes and potentialities.

In my research and teaching, I have found that complexity provides a useful and practical framework for understanding and improving organisational life. As an academic teaching organisation studies, I have found a disjunction, a gaping divide, between everyday work practices and the published organisation-related literature. There appears to be little relationship between the insights of complexity-oriented organisation scholars and the daily work experiences of students. It is apparent that many of those with whom the students work hold limited and outdated ideas about the nature of people and the best ways of inspiring them to get things done. These outdated views tend to favour hierarchical styles of management and compliance of subordinates to superiors. Rather than treating all those involved as autonomous, rational, self-conscious and socially conscious beings, subordinates are often regarded as automatons, only there to enact the intelligence of those higher up in the organisation. My students comment on how intuitively appealing they find a complexity approach, and on how they can use this approach, often in tandem with other theories, to more adequately understand the numerous organising processes they encounter. They also tell me that complexity writing is difficult to engage with, mainly because of its specialised language, which can turn into impenetrable and alien jargon.

I wish to make a supportive argument for complexity theory and thinking. My argument is not just that a complexity approach is 'cutting edge' latest thinking. This in itself is not a compelling enough reason to pursue alternative habits of thinking and doing. There is, I believe, an urgent need for new ways of approaching and engaging with organisational life. At a *local* level the increasing complexity of what is involved – people, differing goals, a changing evolving environment within which organisations interact and concomitantly construct, new forms of technology, alliances and styles of alliance making, and so on – requires suitably sophisticated frameworks of understanding. For example, whereas in the past (for some, but sadly in the present for others) employment in organisations meant that your time was managed for you, with time management itself being used as an instrument of external control, most

1. INTRODUCTION

current employment opportunities now require that you manage and impute a value to your own time. These days you will quite likely be working within, or attempting to manage, organisational processes where some people expect to manage their own time and are highly offended when time is used as an external control, while others are annoyed that you have not given adequate instruction on 'what to do and when'. In an era where the largest proportion of people in post industrialised countries are working with collecting, processing or manipulating information, we need people practised in thoughtfulness and in reasoning, people who are used to employing discriminatory thinking, not people who have learned to wait to be 'told' what to do or think. Yet, how do we maintain a 'together forward' momentum in our organisations as collectives of self-aware, self-directed and psychologically developed people?

> In an era where the largest proportion of people in post industrialised countries are working with collecting, processing or manipulating information, we need people practised in thoughtfulness and in reasoning...

We need to think about changing how we organise ourselves and our organisational structures and institutions. The increasing complexity (complicatedness) implicit in organisational existence requires commensurable sophistication from those involved, especially from those who seek to manage, research or to write about them.

1.2 Being near the edge of chaos

On a *global* scale, we are warned of impending catastrophes, the origins of which implicate human organisations but not just organisations as institutions or corporations where people work. All forms of collective human activity are implicated because all forms of collective activity, from firms and families to religious and political enterprises, are about organisation. All evolve their own preferred and often contested ways of organising collective human behaviour. It seems to me that if imminent catastrophes such as those most notoriously pervasive of awareness and conversation – water shortages, religious wars,

> If imminent catastrophes... are to be limited from becoming biblical in scale, a change of thinking about how we organise ourselves is necessary.

environmental degradation, economic collapse and global temperature change – are to be limited from becoming biblical in scale, a change of thinking about how we organise ourselves is necessary. We need more than mere modifications to the forms of thinking that have brought us to our present situation. We need a different style of thinking, a different paradigmatic perspective. For me, complexity represents such a difference.

In complexity science, the *edge of chaos* describes a specific phenomenon thought to be fundamental to all of nature – to all organic, living entities. In the early 1980s Chris Langdon and Norman Packard each separately discovered that complex adaptive systems naturally move towards a narrow region between fixed behaviour and chaotic behaviour, and that it is in this region that there is *maximum capacity for information computation* (Lewin 1999:54). By translating this revelation to people and their organisations, we can understand that being in this zone of the *edge of chaos* maximises potentiality. With the complexity and associated uncertainty at both local and global scales, the *edge of chaos* is an apt description for where organisations are normally positioned. In this sense, being at the *edge of chaos* is an everyday, moment-by-moment lived experience. Only we prefer to tell ourselves otherwise.

> Being in the zone of the *edge of chaos* maximises potentiality.

If we are too far from the *edge of chaos*, we are doomed to repeat ourselves. There is an organisational colloquialism for this: 'we have a way of doing things here'. If we are too close to the edge, we are fearful and may even come to experience the uncontrolled cascading of events that follow when we cross the *edge of chaos*. Let us then aspire to operate within the zone, *near the edge of chaos*!

> If we are too far from the *edge of chaos*, we are doomed to repeat ourselves.

1.3 From seeing through a lens to seeing the lens

Organisation commentators all share the same beginning point. From someone commenting on their own organisation through to the vast range of organisation-related literature incorporating fads, polished guides on 'how to be successful', erudite theoretical arguments and reports of empirical research studies, there is a common factor: All commentators offer a perspective or view, a certain way of looking at or considering organisational life. Having a perspective is like looking through a lens. Depending on the lens we use (in combination with the kind of eye sight we have) we see different things. Before being given spectacles for my short sightedness, I wondered about the hidden meaning of 'twinkle, twinkle little star'; for me, stars were like small, pale yellow bits of fluff. With my newly acquired specs, they became sparkly. However, when viewing through a telescope, I was, once again, able to see stars differently. Enough of astronomy – this is after all a book about organisations, even if many organisation theorists do tell you to follow one star or another! Many people assume that their way of *seeing*, their way of making sense, or the mental models they hold about organisations, are in some way pure. They believe their views are unsullied by theory – they just see what is there to be seen. Taking this perspective is to fail to recognise that they too are peering through a lens – a lens shaped by their own personal beliefs and theories.

> Many people believe their views are unsullied by theory – they fail to recognise that they too are peering through a lens – a lens shaped by their own personal beliefs and theories.

For example, consider this range of comments given in response to the question 'What is the biggest problem in your organisation?':

'The biggest problem here is incompetent colleagues.'

'Lots of the higher-level managers don't really work; they just do the minimum to appear OK and then work a second job on the sly.'

'The real difficulty is that there isn't enough funding.'

'The problem is that management is incompetent.'

'The problem is we take things too seriously and get too worried about doing our jobs as well as we can.'

'The major difficulty is management taking a matrix approach – it never works and always causes confusion.'

All of these responses relate to the same organisational setting and yet each person's response is different. From each response we know something of the respondent's particular beliefs and theories about how organisations best get things done. For some of them this relates to a certain view of competence in others, for another it is about having enough funds, and for yet another it is the design of the management and reporting processes.

In offering a complexity approach I want to make it clear from the outset that I am offering a perspective – a complexity based lens through which organisational life may be viewed. Here I wish to make clear a separation between the multidimensionality of organisational life, or 'what is', and our ways of thinking about, understanding and theorising this. This perspective is modelled in Figure 1 below. I also hope that, through introducing a complexity approach in the way that I do, I am assisting people in becoming more cognitively agile. That is, more able to draw upon a variety of lenses in their sense making, and having the capacity to do so with awareness.

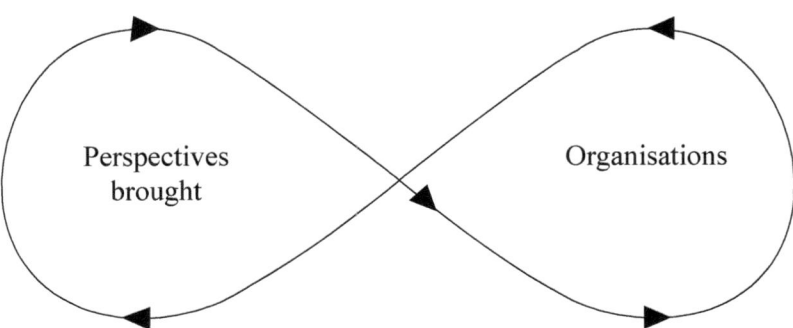

Figure 1
Separation and interconnection between organisations and perspectives (ideas about organisations)

1. INTRODUCTION

1.4 How what goes around changes what comes around

People see or make sense of organisational life in differing ways, in what can be termed a *contested discourse* about organisations. Discourse constitutes conversation on a very large scale. Conversation, both spoken and written, about organisational forms, processes, issues and practices, occurs at multiple sites and between multiple actors. Such conversation between friends, acquaintances and colleagues takes place at work, in corridors, over lunch, at board meetings, symposiums, seminars, through consultants' presentations, in textbooks, scholarly journals and so on.

> ... given that we exist within certain historical, social and cultural contexts, the assumptions we each bring are shaped by our own histories of being and associated communities of belonging.

Discourse about organisational life is described as *contested* because, in this large conversation, there is no overall agreement between and within the range of arguments and opinions offered. What happens is that each conversational contributor brings his or her own assumptions to how they see, with their preconceived ideas shaping what they think they are looking at. Of course, given that we exist within certain historical, social and cultural contexts, the assumptions we each bring are shaped by our own histories of being and associated communities of belonging. Sociologists refer to this as the *social imaginary* within which we exist. This social imaginary is like a cloud of potential surrounding us, but it also establishes limits to what we view as possible. As the educator Paulo Friere (1985:99-100) puts it:

It is not the 'I think' that constitutes the 'we think' but rather the 'we think that makes it possible for me to think'.

Over time, through ongoing debate, a process of change occurs as a result of this interplay between opposing tendencies; we change our views – the social imaginary evolves. Change occurs on a number of fronts. The organisational conversations of which we are part also shape our participation in organisational life, while, at the same time, our experiences within organisations lead us to rethink our beliefs, ideas and theories about our organisations. In other words, there is an ongoing reciprocal interchange between our participation in organisations and our participation in conversations, or theory-building, about organisations. All this influences the ongoing *emergence* of those organisations of which we are part.

By using the term emergence, I mean to emphasise the capacity of organisations to evolve in new and unexpected or unpredictable ways (emergence is more fully introduced in section 2.4.3 in Chapter 2). Emergence describes the way by which complex entities, such as organisations, change or adaptively respond and develop new structures (forms) and characteristics.

As complex entities, organisations exhibit emergence. Organisational life changes; popular and accepted views about how best to understand organisations likewise change. There is circularity here, a mutual evolving of thought and action, described by some theorists as dialectical (in that it is a process of change that proceeds from interplay between opposing tendencies) and reciprocal (in that action influences thought and thought influences action).

In Figure 2 overleaf, I model some indicative examples of this process.

> The organisational conversations of which we are part also shape our participation in organisational life, while, at the same time, our experiences within organisations lead us to rethink our beliefs, ideas and theories about our organisations.

1. INTRODUCTION

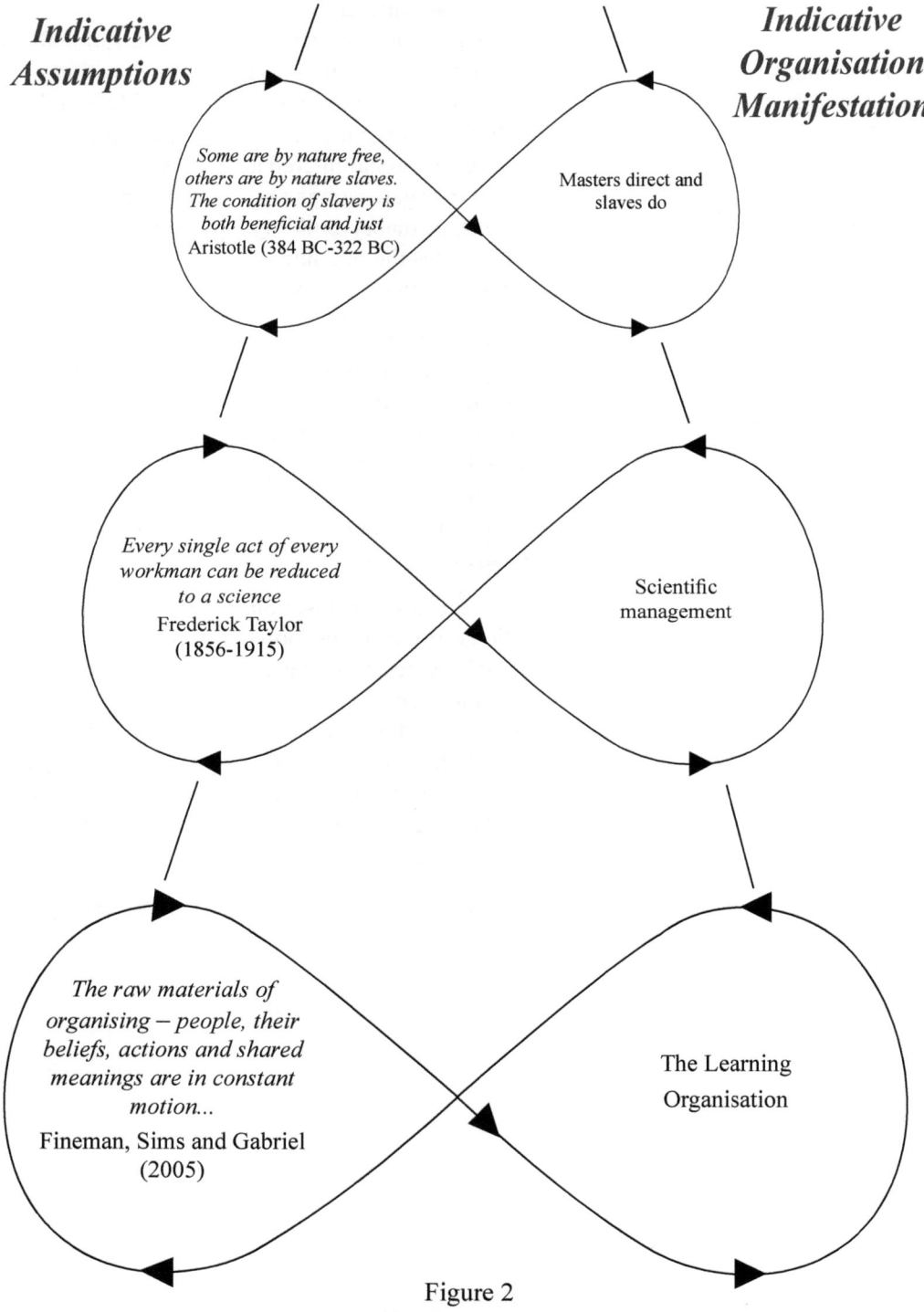

Figure 2
Examples of the dialectical and reciprocal
process of evolving thought and action

We are all living at the *edge of chaos*. We have no guarantees that those corporations and institutions where we work will continue to exist in their present forms. We have no guarantee that those natural environmental processes on which life itself depends will continue to exist in present forms. We have no guarantees that those cultural and social norms about us will not change. Actually, our accumulated intelligence amasses evidence that, as Heraclitus (536-470BC) remarked so many centuries ago, all is change, we live within perpetual flux: *You cannot step twice into the same river; for fresh waters are ever flowing in upon you* (Russell 1995:63). With ongoing change, there is a 'real and present danger' of chaos erupting as we try to cope with challenges to our present forms of being and doing – organising.

1.5 What can a complexity view offer?

Looking through a complexity lens we see organisations as comprising a number of interacting self-organising, dynamic and emergent entities, not least of which are people. It can only be expected, then, that organisations must also exist as self-organising, dynamic and emergent entities. Given that organisations continuously interact with other people and organisations, and that these interactions are mutually influencing, it is soon clear that organisations manifest their emergence within a complex milieu. In short, complexity views individuals, organisations, populations and environments as interrelating, self-organising, dynamic and emergent; they are messy, unpredictable and small changes potentially have major consequences.

So far, I have depicted complexity as describing a world of uncertainty and contingency, arising from interactions amongst self-organising, dynamic and emergent entities. I have not as yet made an enticing argument for valuing complexity as useful in understanding organisations. A complexity approach is useful however, in that it does three things:

> ... complexity views individuals, organisations, populations and environments as interrelating, self-organising, dynamic and emergent; they are messy, unpredictable and small changes potentially have major consequences.

1. INTRODUCTION

1. It removes simplistic hopes of an ordered and controllable existence where, if only we had the right 'keys' or 'tools', we could fashion organisations to our own image and dreams and thus ensure 'success' (meaning, perhaps, a flourishing sustainability of our organisation).
2. It offers a means of discerning and identifying underlying patterns of order, thus providing a richer understanding and appreciation of situations (or processes), as well as indicators for influencing future emergences.
3. It introduces us to *potentiality* (possible future emergences) by showing how simple recurrent rules result in complex behaviour and emergence. While systems or entities (such as individual people or organisations) may exist in various states (having multiple potentialities), complexity shows how the state that unfolds is the result of interactive local relationships. We can come to understand this potentiality and in certain cases may learn to influence it. However, we also need to realise that 'influential interventions' do not take a neat cause-and-effect path but may generate unexpected self-organising behaviour and emergent outcomes. This takes us back to point 1. above, and the thinking starts again!

Let me demonstrate the value of complexity with a simple example. Take the situation of a rebellious teenager and his parents. Psychology informs us that it is normal and necessary for children to rebel, to find ways of separating themselves from their parents and so grow into adulthood. As a parent, I can endeavour to control my child, perhaps because I may be concerned that he will become a delinquent engaging in activities not to my taste or dangerous to himself and others. I have found that taking a tightly controlling stance often results in teenagers rebelling all the more. My child and I self-organise as we respond to one another and a heavy-handed approach may be felt by the child to be a direct imposition on his self-organising capacity. He may then choose a stronger means of enacting and demonstrating his capacity to self-organise. So, a heavy-handed approach may have the opposite effect to what I had hoped for. When my son was a teenager, I decided that he could do anything with his hair. Not that I told him this in so many words, but I supported his various experiments in appearance, concluding, (I think), with him having his hair dyed bright blue for his twenty-first birthday. My son loved having a 'cool' mum in this regard. My idea was that hairstyle was no big deal and that if he channelled 'rebellious' instincts in this direction, he would not need, perhaps, to become rebellious in ways that did concern me. This story is an example of where understanding the larger patterns (that people are self-organising, dynamic and emergent beings who act in accord with their own internal logic; that children have a need for separation and self expression) means that I can behave in a way that may influence or nudge in, what was for me, a positive direction. I was not controlling outcomes or behaviour. Nor was I giving up the power to influence events. Rather I could take a quieter, humble approach that allowed my son and I to remain not at odds, but in a coherent relationship with one another. However, situations are always more complex than we comprehend. My son's employer at the time did not take a complexity view of his blue hair. She thought blue hair was inappropriate for someone who worked with people with disabilities. He had to recolour it or leave! I do not, however, recall that changing the colour of one's hair was written into his contract as grounds for dismissal. His hair colour did not impact on his capacity to sensitively care for his clients, many of whom enjoyed the novelty of it.

In organisational life, we may see echoes of the patterns discerned above. Having one's working life tightly controlled often results in resentment and attempts at disempowering 'the system' or 'supervisor', rather than in feeling respected and treated like a thoughtful human being who is keen to contribute to a joint enterprise. Those rebellious tendencies of our teenage years stay with us in some measure and may be brought fully to life in certain situations. Overly zealous attempts to control, in failing to recognise the inherent self-organising, dynamic and emergent characteristics of human beings, may generate unexpected and undesired outcomes.

> Having one's working life tightly controlled often results in resentment and attempts at disempowering 'the system' or 'supervisor', rather than in feeling respected and treated like a thoughtful human being... .

1. INTRODUCTION

1.6 The shape of this book

Fractal fragments, as stories, narrative accounts, or case studies about organisational life, are used throughout this book as practical examples to illustrate the theoretical material. While in Chapter 3 I describe the nature of fractals and *fractality* in greater detail, I want to give some explanation here so that you will understand what is implied when I write of fractal fragments. Complex entities or systems, which are the focus of this book, unfold in fractal dimensions. For example, we see fractal dimensions where the forking of a tree trunk is repeated in the forking of large branches, right through to the forking of the tiniest twigs on the same tree. The term *fractal* is used here to describe phenomena that show similarities across different scales of focus. Similarly, when the eighteenth century English poet William Blake writes *To see a World in a Grain of Sand,* he is describing the whole world and a grain of sand as being organised fractally; there are indications about the whole world in just one grain of sand. I call my examples to demonstrate theoretical material *fractal fragments* because I believe the experiences described in these are indicative of the organisational experiences of many people in many different roles and across many different sites. Part of the usefulness of *fractality* is that examination at one scale of focus yields information about the structure and related characteristics of the whole. Examining one fractal component at one scale enables you to thereby manage what would otherwise be overwhelming detail.

> Part of the usefulness of *fractality* is that examination at one scale of focus yields information about the structure and related characteristics of the whole.

The narratives on which most of these fractal fragments are based were collected through a research project where a range of people, working in different styles of organisation, were interviewed and invited to relate telling stories about the practices by which their organisation typically 'gets things done'. A couple of fractal fragments are drawn from recent research collaborations between colleagues, specific organisations and myself. The identity of some participants and their organisations has been camouflaged to protect anonymity. However, other participants were pleased to have themselves and their organisations presented in this book.

Complexity concepts or metaphors are introduced and demonstrated as 'tools' for developing new insights and understandings of the organisational forms, processes, practices, issues and problems highlighted through the fractal fragments. It is intended that, through this process, complexity habits of thought will be demonstrated in an accessible manner.

Following this Introduction, Chapter 2 discusses the basic terms of reference: complexity, organisations and organising. The major organising principles of complexity – self-organisation, dynamism and emergence – are introduced and related to current presentation of organisational and management issues. Fractal fragment (1) is presented and analysed using these principles and the complexity metaphor, *fitness landscape*, is introduced.

Chapter 3 introduces and explains specific complexity metaphors, demonstrating their use as tools for better understanding and improving organisational life. The seven metaphors introduced are: *fitness landscape, phase space – phrase space, communicative connectedness, sensitive dependence on initial conditions, edge of chaos – chaotic edge, attractors* and *fractality*. How each metaphor can be used in organisational settings is demonstrated with reference to fractal fragment (3). The chapter concludes with the presentation of fractal fragment (4) and its complexity-based analysis.

Chapter 4 introduces three complexity-based inquiry methods: *Coherent Conversations, Fractal Analysis* and *Attractor Analysis*. Illustrative analytical descriptions are then developed for a final three fractal fragments, demonstrating how applied complexity-based pattern analysis helps identify underlying patterns of order and indications of future possible emergences. It concludes with a description of two ways of working with complexity that draw together complexity habits of thought and philosophical, psychological and sociological insights. The first presents *identity, access to resources* and *will to powe*r as a universal human *attractor* set. The second explores ethical implications of human self-organisation.

1. INTRODUCTION

Chapter 5 'Organising at the *edge of chaos*' brings a partial and temporary conclusion to the adventures in complexity as set out in this book. I say partial and temporary because the ideas that I have presented in this book are only part of a conversation. Your ways of engaging, your critical and creative responses, carry the adventure forward and so, in a sense, the uncertainty of the outcome of the adventure remains a potentiality within those so involved.

> Utilising complexity habits of thought is radically different from just adding a few new words and concepts to old ways of thinking.

The book moves from discussion of principles through to specifics. The reason for this is that what is most important is not learning some new complexity terms, such as *edge of chaos*, but understanding the intellectual sense-making framework and learning about complexity habits of thought. My aim is that this book helps you to gain access to complexity mediational means (Vygotsky 1978); in other words, that you are able to utilise complexity-mediated ways of making sense. Utilising complexity habits of thought is radically different from just adding a few new words and concepts to old ways of thinking.

Further Reading

About Organisations
Fineman, S., Sims, D. and Gabriel, Y. (2005) *Organizing and organizations.* London: Sage.

Introduction to complexity
Lewin, R. (1999) *Complexity, life at the edge of chaos.* Chicago: University of Chicago Press.

Philosophically Interesting
Friere, P. (1985) *The politics of education.* (Trans. Donaldo Macedo) Mass.: Bergin and Garvey.

Russell, B. (1995) *History of western philosophy.* New York: Routledge.

Psychologically Interesting
Vygotsky, L. (1978) *Mind in society: the development of higher psychological processes.* Cambridge: Harvard University Press.

2. ORGANISATIONS AND COMPLEXITY

2.1 *Fractal fragment (1) Jay and Bilal, Outreach Loans Bank*

During my research I met with two mobile lenders for a branchless bank. I found the story about their experiences in working for Outreach Loans Bank fascinating. In many ways their narrative depicts common work experiences and, as such, it provides a useful starting place for explaining 1) the basic organising principles of a complexity framework and 2) a complexity approach to studying organisations. I will begin this chapter by telling you about Jay and Bilal and their employment with Outreach Loans Bank. This Outreach Loans Bank fractal fragment will then be drawn upon as I introduce a complexity paradigm and major complexity organising principles.

Jay and Bilal explained that their employment required them to visit people directly in their homes or workplaces, rather than working out of a branch. Both are enthusiastic about their jobs. *'I like to be able to work autonomously, and being an Outreach Loans Officer means it's like owning my own business. There isn't anyone looking over my shoulder – we are given a great deal of responsibility for managing what we do. Although we all have the same job description we need flexibility because of the nature of making appointments. I think we are harder working than if we had to go into an office every day,'* stated Jay. Bilal added, *'I like having a home office, not being stuck in a large office from 9 - 5, and going out and meeting people everyday. To do this job well you need to be part of the community. Having a distinctively marked vehicle and clothing and visiting people in their workplace or home gives us a local presence. This job provides a lifestyle that I like'*.

Each Outreach Loans Officer reports directly to the Bank's Sales Officer. Every week they complete an Excel spreadsheet and once a month they attend meetings of all Loans Officers. Officers are paid a base salary and are assigned individual targets that, if met, give them a bonus at the end of each quarter. *'The bonus system works well – mostly it means that there is a clear relationship between how much you work and how much bonus you get. But sometimes you think you'll meet the target and things fall down. If all goes well and your client is having a satisfying and happy experience then you'll reach your target. Occasionally, though, for other reasons, the client no longer wants to take the loan and unless you are following up a number of leads, this might mean you don't make the target,'* explained Jay.

Working autonomously requires a high degree of self-responsibility. As Jay put it: *'When you're working autonomously you still have to front up to work each day. You're responsible for everything. Where's your stationary come from? You've got to buy it. If you run out, that affects your work - you can't do things for your clients. You have to do all the menial tasks. You're secretary, typist and administrator! You've got to have your office sorted out, have it clean, have confidential documents securely stored and ensure you comply with governance and Occupational Health and Safety regulations. Being professional means I don't conduct business sitting in my pyjamas in the lounge, with clients' papers scattered around.'*

> Working autonomously requires a high degree of self-responsibility.

'Yes,' commented Bilal, *'it means paying attention to how we manage our workspace - which includes the car. We are always in the public eye. We are always representing the company. The car is decaled; we wear a distinctive uniform. It means if I go out at night with my friends I have to be very careful about who goes in my car. If one of my passengers wolf whistles at a girl then this could mean instant dismissal for me. But on the other hand people often come up to you when you are out, so having the car is advertising and it helps create extra business.'*

While finding the job exciting and having excellent support from the company, Jay and Bilal are also acutely aware of some difficulties. *'I think I am*

2. ORGANISATIONS AND COMPLEXITY

borderline edge of chaos. Sometimes I take on too much and I can have a sense of nearly going over the edge, when things don't work for reasons beyond my control,' reflected Bilal. *'Yes,'* agreed Jay, *'Bilal probably doesn't have a calm existence. But I'm a little different. Because I've been working autonomously for 20 years, I make conscious decisions to move the glass away from the edge of the table. I can tell when I need to take certain actions to stop my situation from getting too chaotic and difficult.'*

'Another difficulty is that because you are not on site in head office, there is often an 'us and them' attitude from other departments. It means it can be frustrating trying to get information that you need, especially if the individual you're engaging with is not client-focused', offered Bilal. *'That culture is in all companies. It's because the people in the office are stuck working all day in discomfort, only able to take breaks at regulated intervals, and, over time, an institutional culture takes over,'* advised Jay.

'It's a good exciting job. But I miss the social side of a workplace, like going with colleagues for Friday night drinks or having an office Christmas party,' concluded Bilal.

2.2   *Introducing a complexity paradigm*

I now take a theoretical turn to introduce a complexity paradigm and the major organising principles of complexity. Fractal fragment (1) will be returned to, from time to time, to provide practical, grounded illustrations of theoretical material.

So, to introduce complexity. A complexity (short for complexity science or theory) perspective represents the beginnings of a new *paradigm*. A paradigm, in essence, describes a situation where a set of concepts, beliefs or philosophies is shared by a group of people. Under the title of 'complexity' can be grouped a newly emerging (if you think concepts developed over the past 50 years are new) set of concepts and basic assumptions about the nature and organisation of the

> Under the title of 'complexity' can be grouped a newly emerging (if you think concepts developed over the past 50 years are new) set of concepts and basic assumptions about the nature and organisation of the world...

world, derived from studying dynamical systems in domains such as physics, mathematics, computing and biology. This identifiable set of understandings provides a way of thinking and a way of seeing – a paradigmatic framing of our sense making. Complexity constitutes a paradigm because it describes a set of concepts shared by a community of scholars. These scholars can be said to be more or less peering through the same lens and sharing in the same social imaginary. Those holding to a complexity paradigm discern patterns in certain phenomena that otherwise appear as chaotic (Wolfram 2002; Kauffman 1995), and recognise that complex systems, comprising many independent interacting variables, balance order and chaos, maintaining themselves in a zone – *the edge of chaos.*

> Complexity constitutes a paradigm because it describes a set of concepts shared by a community of scholars. These scholars can be said to be more or less peering through the same lens and sharing in the same social imaginary.

These communities of people extend beyond the areas named above. A wide ranging group of scholars and practitioners have begun engaging with and developing complexity related concepts, exploring and evolving complexity approaches to economics, education, health, innovation, psychology, management, organisation studies and so on. Complexity-focussed national and international conferences have been held for more than ten years. There are specialist complexity organisation consultants, a large and growing number of books elaborating complexity approaches to various aspects of studying organisations, and even a journal, *Emergence,* dedicated to exploring complexity applications and insights to organisations and management.

> ... when I write of complexity... I am referring to specific ways of discerning pattern and order out of the multidimensionality of existence.

So when I write of complexity I do not mean complicated. In a paradigmatic sense, I am referring to specific ways of discerning pattern and order out of the multidimensionality of existence.

In a book about organisations, why should we become so philosophical and theoretical? My response is that, as discussed in Chapter 1, this is what people do all of the time; we make sense of things, discerning pattern and order out of the multidimensionality of existence, through preferred lenses or frameworks. We do this within communities of like-minded people but, most of the time, we are not aware that this is what we are doing.

In contrast to a complexity perspective, many people who study organisations take what can be called a positivist perspective in their discerning of pattern and order. This positivist perspective constitutes a widely accepted paradigm within management and organisation studies. People taking this view see *an observable, objective organisational reality which exists independent of organisation theory* (Grey 2005:6). The task of theory from a positivist perspective is to uncover this separate reality. People interested in how to manage organisations more effectively often take a positivist perspective, linking together *the goal of providing fact-based, reliable organisational predictions* (Grey 2005:5) with their assumptions that the goals of managers are legitimate, that value-neutral data can be securely attained and that organisational prediction and control are possible. Such goals and assumptions are likely to come out of a view that sees 'the reality' of organisational life as comprising a hierarchy which privileges the interests of managers over those of 'workers', and 'reality' as predictable and controllable. This view differs radically from the complexity perspective of this book.

2.3 *Organising or arranging: what's the difference?*

I want to make a distinction between organising and arranging. Inorganic objects such as mobile phones, computers or statues can be arranged. A collection of mobile phones can be sorted according to colour, size or capability. Changing how the mobile phones are placed in an arrangement has no effect on each phone. Similarly, each may be taken apart and subsequently the component parts may be reassembled. If done correctly, the phone itself will not have been adversely affected. However, organisations are human enterprises and are highly reliant upon those involved and their favoured and habitual ways of making sense of and engaging with others. Relationships and communication really matter. Organisations exist

2. ORGANISATIONS AND COMPLEXITY

... individuals and human organisations are complex – they are not reducible to component parts, and are forever influencing and being influenced: they are inherently relational.

through, or as, various processes of organising activity undertaken by socially interacting individuals, each employing various frames of reference. How they relate to and communicate with each other affects the organising processes while at the same time affecting those individuals involved. In working together – organising – we influence one another. Ross Ashby, neuroscientist, mathematician and early progenitor of complexity, argued in the 1960s that central to the concept of organisation (in relation to living systems) is 'conditionality':

As soon as the relation between two entities A and B becomes conditional on C's value or state then a necessary component of 'organisation' is present. (Ashby 1962:255-56)

Bilal and Jay's situation and experiences clearly show conditionality. For example, the relation between Jay, an Outreach Loans Officer, and his client is conditional upon the client requiring a loan, the rules of Australia and the Outreach Loans Bank guiding loan funding protocols, the participation of Head Office staff and so on.

More generally, considering the multiple relationships between people, teams, departments or firms, we can imagine how the relationships in any business or not-for-profit organisation would be conditional upon something else. This something else could be the quality of the context of the relationship (a strict hierarchical bureaucracy, friendly competitors etc.), financial status and so on.

Ashby goes to the heart of what is involved in human organisations and processes of organising: that we are always in situations where the relation between 'entities' (be these people, processes, policies or strategies) is conditional, influenced by something else such as other people, processes, contexts and so on. In this sense, individuals and human organisations are complex – they are not reducible to component parts, and are forever influencing and being influenced: they are inherently relational.

2. ORGANISATIONS AND COMPLEXITY

Sometimes, in organisational life, people appear to assume that other people, or organisational forms and processes, are mere arrangements and are not dependent upon multiple relationships and interactions. This causes problems. For example, when someone criticises you and they begin by saying '*Don't take this personally but…*' their criticism usually does hurt – it is personal in nature. However, your critic seems to assume or hope that you will not have your sense of self challenged by their comment because it is meant in a 'professional' or 'purely objective' way. But we are persons, and the criticism invariably is of our person. This experience may well go on to colour all future interactions with this person, and even with others we interact with that day (just don't take it out on your dog). Conversely, we may not be touched at all by the interaction. Either way, relationships are critical to ongoing interactions within the organisation.

> Arrangement thinking is also evidenced when people are moved into and out of various positions in the organisation with little consideration given to the ripple effect generated through the multiple relationships being implicated by the change.

Arrangement thinking is also evidenced when people are moved into and out of various positions in the organisation with little consideration given to the ripple effect generated through the multiple relationships being implicated by the change. Not only can this affect knowledge management, as has been well recognised, but there may be other implications, such as emotional impacts of the change, on all those affected. Being moved, I might ask – 'Is this a promotion or a demotion for me? Does this mean what I do and how I do it is valued or not valued?' A change in position may mean moving house, prompting further changes – 'Now I'll have to find a new school for my children, and in this area education is far more expensive! But I don't get a pay rise, so I'm not happy about this'. Having a different colleague with whom to liaise might have another person grumbling – 'I don't understand her way of communicating'.

Fractal fragment (1) illustrates conditionality in an organisational setting. The capacity of the Outreach Loans Bank to function successfully is conditional upon an almost infinite number of relationships. For example, the functioning of the Bank is related to activities of existing and emerging competitors, changes in government rules, population growth, cultural norms and expectations (for example, whether it is thought to be OK to take out loans through such banks) and so on.

> Organising is viewed as a continuous and emergent activity involving ongoing processes of relating between people, personalities, preferences, politics and power.

At every level of organisational functioning, conditionality is present, with each entity (person, group, division and so on) relating within situations of mutual influence. Complexity as a theoretical framework is characterised by the idea that *everything is related to everything else*. Complexity assumes radical relationality – that *nothing is without being in relation and that everything is in the way it is – in terms and in virtue of relationality* (Dillon 2000:4). So, in studying forms and processes of organising from a complexity perspective, there is no clear cut-off point where we can say 'but that doesn't relate to the study of organisations'. It means big picture thinking, relating ideas from philosophy, anthropology, sociology, psychology and much more. Organising is viewed as a continuous and emergent activity involving ongoing processes of relating between people, personalities, preferences, politics and power. Organising is, of course, a self-organising, dynamic and emergent process. It is as much a personal process involving our emotions and preferred sense-making stories (narratives) as it is a social process, with actions, beliefs and meanings all in motion and evolving.

2.4 A complexity cosmography

> A *complexity cosmography* sets out the main features of a complexity way of thinking about and describing the nature of the world, people and organisations.

This section introduces a *complexity cosmography* – it describes the basic organising principles of a complexity framework. Explanation of these principles will make clear how a complexity view offers different habits of thinking to those derived from linear, objective, positivist accounts that have so dominated the literature of organisation studies. Cosmography, from the Greek word *kosmographia* meaning 'description of the world', is the science concerned with describing and mapping the main features of the heavens and earth, or universe. A complexity cosmography thus sets out the main features of a complexity way of thinking about and describing the nature of the world, people and organisations.

Perhaps, rather than complexity cosmography, I could write that I am outlining a *complexity paradigm* because, in describing the main features of a complexity way of thinking, I am describing a set of concepts shared by a community of scholars or scientists. Perhaps I should write of a *complexity world view* because I am describing a philosophy and interpretation of the world held by myself and other complexity theorists. However, neither paradigm nor world view focusses on outlining the set of concepts, beliefs or assumptions that are shared.

A complexity cosmography construes a world that is *self-organising, dynamic* and *emergent*. Self-organisation, dynamism (adaptability) and emergence were recognised early on by complexity researchers who referred variously to 'complex self-organising systems', 'complex adaptive systems' and 'complex emergent systems'.

> Both individuals and organisations interact with, and exist within, contexts or environments that are self-organising, dynamic and emergent.

Individuals and organisations are seen to comprise a number of interacting self-organising, dynamic and emergent systems. For individuals these include cells, organs and immunological, skeletal and respiratory systems and so forth. For organisations, we have committees, working parties, sections, divisions and so on. Both individuals and organisations interact with, and exist within, contexts or environments that are self-organising, dynamic and emergent. A recent article 'Seeking a husband? Get a degree' in *The Sydney Morning Herald* (Monday April 7 2008) gives an example of self-organisation, dynamics and emergence. The article reports the research findings of Genevieve Heard of the Centre for Population and Urban Research at Monash University. Her analysis of the 2006 census shows that women with degrees are more likely to marry than those without. Only ten years earlier, in the 1996 census, the opposite was the case and women without university degrees had higher marriage rates; if we go back around 100 years, we find that women did not attend universities in Australia. Other countries' histories replicate this experience, with minor modifications. So, over time, choices and expectations about higher education for women have changed and these changes have affected marriage rates.

2.4.1 Self-organisation

Self-organisation refers to the capacity of complex living systems (such as a goldfish, you and me, my cat, the firm in which you are employed) to evolve into organised forms according to internally evolving principles. People evolve through interactions with their environments, including other people, according to internally driven responses. Our capacity to change form (metamorphose) while continuing to be ourselves is self-organisation in action. We maintain ourselves as ourselves over time and through many different experiences. Similarly, households, families, neighbourhoods, businesses, cities, nations, cultures and so on, all are involved in the ongoing creation and metamorphosing of themselves through processes of self-organisation.

Jay and Bilal, employees of the Outreach Loans Bank, each self-organise. How each loans officer arranges his/her home office space, daily appointments and weekly schedules, maintains his/her vehicle, keeps records, develops relationships with clients, colleagues and supervisors, reacts to criticism or praise, all implicate self-organisation.

Slime mould (*Dictyostelium discordeum*), that rarely thought-of slippery reddish-orange stuff found in damp, dark places, provides a wonderful example of self-organisation. Evelyn Fox Keller (Johnson 2001) found that slime mould oscillates between being a single organism (comprised of a single cell) and a swarm of distinct cells, depending on the condition of its environment. Evidently, slime mould spends much of its life as thousands of distinct single-celled units, each moving separately. However, when conditions are inhospitable, the slime mould coalesces into a single large organism. Without having an identified leader, aggregation is triggered by alterations in the amount of a substance called 'cyclic AMP' released by each cell. When conditions are less hospitable cyclic AMP is released and each of the cells then follow the pheromone trial encountered, thus creating clusters of cells. The 'they' becomes 'it'.

The triggering of slime mould towards forming a single large entity or a myriad of single cells constitutes self-organisation. Each cell is self-organising and yet 'local' relationships and interactions result in some kind of discernable macro behaviour. Johnson argues that slime mould behaviour provides a metaphor for understanding how change occurs in an array of complex entities, from brains through to cities. The principles are 1) that change occurs (external and internal) when self-organising entities self-organise in certain ways in response to their environment and 2) that local connections or relationships are critical.

When I am giving a seminar I am starkly reminded that people are innately self-organising. No matter what I say, or what efforts I put into making my presentation clear and convincing, I have no control over how my audience will respond. Will they relate to what I say? Will they have listened to me, or might they have been thinking about some issue of far more personal importance? I was surprised, once, when, at the beginning of my lecture, I asked the students about their understanding of the meaning of 'discourse'. One sincerely helpful young man told me it meant being 'off course' or going in the wrong direction. His answer represented his self-organised response to my introduction of an unfamiliar term, with an attempt to make sense of it within his conceptual framework. His assessment of the situation demonstrated another aspect of his self-organisation – he judged that the environment was safe enough for him to risk giving an incorrect response, and that someone responding would help the session move along. Further, to produce speech his body self-organised by adequately organising interactions between the neural processes underlying language formulation and speech planning and the systems of speech production (such as respiration, phonation, articulation).

The functioning of organisations is reliant upon and emerges from ongoing interactions and forms of accommodation between self-organising entities. Some organisational procedures and processes, such as those of Outreach Loans Bank, allow for and work with the natural self-organising capacities of the organisation's employees, thereby facilitating greater coherence between the self-organising capacities of employees and the organisation. Other organisational processes frustrate people's self-organising tendencies. Recall the comments of Anna, from the National Counselling Service (fractal fragment (2)):

'Our organisation is very hierarchical. I'm answerable to my boss, and he's answerable to his, and his boss is answerable to the board. So the way we get things done is by this hierarchical chain. It means poor communication and poor information dissemination. If I have concerns and want decisions made, I discuss these with my boss at our monthly meetings. I then have to wait for him to take the matter to his boss, who then takes it to the board. Everything takes a long time because we are so hierarchical.'

With long waits for decisions, Anna self-organises to manage the delays. She develops tactics for clarifying her requests, so that there is less chance of the request being poorly communicated up and down the hierarchical management structure.

Anna sees her counselling section of this organisation as having a more uninhibited capacity to self-organise. She clearly describes the way in which her section self-organises in response to ongoing perturbations from changes occurring elsewhere within the organisation:

'I think that as a counselling service we are self-organising and I see that in each level there are limits and within these I have incredible freedom. Barring budgets and staff hours, I have freedom to organise how we do what we do. And it's always changing. The minute there's a change from the hierarchy I need to

communicate it. Or we come up against an issue and so we need to change.'

In both organisational settings, Outreach Loans Bank and the National Counselling Service, the people involved self-organise, for this is the nature of complex systems. Understanding this principle provides insights into the implications of various organisation structural arrangements, processes and procedures. In viewing people and organisations as inherently self-organising, the focus moves from prediction and control to the development of structural arrangements, processes and procedures. These enhance a climate that is conducive to coherence between the self-organisation of the individual, team, section, division and the whole organisation.

2.4.2 Dynamism

Complexity considers *dynamism* to be an essential characteristic of life. To be dynamic is to be adaptive, to have energy, to instigate, to respond and react. The descriptor *dynamic* refers to the continuous movement of all entities as they adapt, respond to and influence others and the environment (social and physical) within which they exist.

Complexity's emphasis on the dynamism of the world marks one of its distinguishing features from classical science. Rather than emphasise stability in the form of optimum states of entities or systems, complexity expects ongoing adaptability. This perspective is well suited to working with people and institutions. The functioning of an organisation depends upon interactions and accommodations between self-organising entities (individual people as well as teams, divisions etc.). Both dynamism and self-organisation emphasise that context and circumstances change for all, and that all 'things' (people, environments, organisations and so on) are in continuous flux. Further, these changes may be different in time, scale and importance for each of those who are interacting.

> Rather than emphasise stability in the form of optimum states of entities or systems, complexity expects ongoing adaptability.

Consider the collapse of the Icelandic economy in 2008. In 2007 the economy appeared strong, with Iceland rated as having the fourth highest gross

> Both dynamism and self-organisation emphasise that context and circumstances change for all, and that all 'things' (people, environments, organisations and so on) are in continuous flux.

domestic product per capita in the world and an unemployment rate of between 0 and 1% (*Sydney Morning Herald* 10 November 2008). By October 2008, however, Icelandic banks were in trouble. Rapid and disastrous changes were taking place, as evidenced by Prime Minister Geir Haarde's statement: *'As recently as last night it looked like the banks could continue operations for a while. This morning and today, things have totally changed for the worse'*. In an attempt to save the whole country from financial ruin, his government instituted an emergency bill allowing the government to take control of the nation's banks, *enabling it to push through mergers between banks or force them into bankruptcy* (*The Guardian Weekly* 10 October 2008). Despite this action, people lost their savings, experienced cuts in salary or loss of employment and businesses went under. Exchange rates fell from 65 krona to the US dollar in 2007 to 130 krona in November 2008. And the dynamism continues, with ongoing adaptations and responses fanning out from individuals through to nations and beyond.

Dynamism as adaptability can mean something more than merely interacting and reacting. People do not only discern patterns but they can learn about this process: how to do something differently and more effectively, which patterns are more useful than others, how to communicate ideas with others and so on. In other words, we learn through experience and self-adapt as a result.

Dynamism is demonstrated at multiple levels in the Outreach Loans Bank fractal fragment. Interactions within socially, politically and economically evolving environments require a capacity to respond and react. Jay and Bilal's daily work of interacting with clients, colleagues and supervisors cannot help but be characterised by dynamism and demonstrates the ability to react and respond. Jay described how, being more experienced, he has learnt (adapted) to better manage the dynamism of their work:

'Bilal probably doesn't have a calm existence. But I'm a little different. Because I've been working autonomously for 20 years, I make conscious decisions to move the glass away from the edge of the table. I can tell when I need to take certain actions to stop my situation from getting too chaotic and difficult.'

At another level of the Bank, dynamism is seen in relation to the way that the Bank's finances are managed. As has been painfully apparent recently, dynamism in international money markets is continuous and at times volatile. An American credit crisis, as reported in the international paper the Guardian Weekly (10-16 October 2008), can quickly become a *Financial contagion [that] threatens the eurozone.* A small locally owned bank would not be immune from these influences. Such fluctuations in international money markets generate a range of effects, one of which might be that Outreach Loans Bank raises its interest rates. Or it may be that the Bank itself has difficulties in operating and it retrenches employees, with Outreach Loans Officers like Jay and Bilal ending up unemployed.

2.4.3 Emergence

There are three important points to be made about *emergence*. The first is that emergence refers to the capacity of complex entities to exhibit unexpected and novel properties or behaviours not previously observed as functional characteristics of the complex entity. As Morgan, way back in 1927, stated:

The emphasis is not on the unfolding of something already in being but on the outspringing of something that has hitherto not been in being. (Morgan 1927:112)

The second point is that the term emergence carries with it the idea that micro-phenomena give rise to macro-phenomena, with characteristics observed in the macro-phenomena not being reducible to the micro-phenomena.

The third point is more difficult to explain. It relates specifically to the role of humans in co-constructing the phenomena of which they are part. Emergence, as described thus far, locates the outspringing of something new as a concrete capacity of the complex entity under observation. In this sense, emergence is taken to be a behaviour or event of the complex entity itself.

However, there are debates amongst complexity scientists as to what properly constitutes emergence. Some argue that the term emergence may only correctly be applied when things happen that are not at all predictable, that utterly surprise us. However, such a distinction is problematic because the mindset of the observer is not taken into account. Is something thought to emerge simply because we do not have the particular way of observing that would have picked up earlier indications of the emergent phenomena?

One way of responding to this dilemma is to gloss over it (making a general point that when dealing with people this distinction is not really so important) and to accept in principle that because of their self-organising, self-reflective capacities and complex characters, people are more likely than not to behave as emergent beings and to surprise not only others but themselves as well. Envisioned in this way, it is very easy to think of experiences of emergence in the social realm. In a mundane sense, many adults when asked about their life experiences will say 'I never expected to experience.... (being a parent, not becoming a parent, being divorced, getting cancer, winning an Academy award)' and so on. A student recently told me of her sense of personal emergence over the past few years. She said that, as a consequence of getting a job in the human resources section of a company, she thought she would benefit from some qualifications and enrolled in the Bachelor of Business degree in which I teach. She now finds herself utterly fascinated by psychology and plans to begin studying for a degree next year after she has completed her present course of study. Five years ago this interest was unknown to her. Now it has become her passion!

This third point about emergence, however, recognises emergence in human settings as a phenomenon that conjointly comes into being through the interplay between the situation and human sense-making capacities. It relates to the understanding described in the introduction (and demonstrated in Figure 2) whereby organisations and theorising about organisations was shown as a dialectical and reciprocal process: the organisational conversations of which we are part shaping our participation in organisational life, and the experiences in participation leading to modifications of our beliefs, theories and conversations. Implications for organisational life, through this way of understanding emergence, will be elaborated further at the conclusion of this section.

The second point, that complex phenomena and behaviours emerge from simpler phenomena, has been demonstrated through computer simulations. Wolfram (2002), in working with this medium to replicate the behaviours of complex organic entities, found that just by following very simple rules he could obtain forms of great complexity. As an example, Wolfram shows how the complexity of a plant can be traced through to very simple rules guiding growth at the tip of the stem of the plant.

...consider the stem of a plant. It is usually only at the tip of a stem that growth can occur, and much of the time all that ever happens is that the stem just gets progressively longer. But the crucial phenomenon that ultimately leads to much of the structure we see in many kinds of plants is that at the tip of a stem it is possible for new stems to form and branch off. And in the simplest cases these new stems are in essence just smaller copies of the original stem, with the same basic rules for growth and branching.
(Wolfram 2002:400)

Here we have the complexity of a plant characterized as emerging out of repeated simple rules guiding growth behaviour at the tip of each stem of the plant.

This idea, of something simpler generating something more complex, can be summarised as

2. ORGANISATIONS AND COMPLEXITY

micro-phenomena giving rise to macro-phenomena. What is really interesting is that the emergent macro-phenomena has properties, substances and behaviours that are novel and cannot be deduced from even the most complete knowledge of the micro-phenomena and its fundamental properties, substances and behaviours.

Let us pause a moment and return to the Outreach Loans Bank fractal fragment. How is emergence shown here? That Outreach Loans Bank operates as a branchless bank is itself an emergent outcome. Not having branches is a strategy that evolved to provide a competitive advantage over banks configured as branch systems. Perhaps the simple rules guiding this emergence were that Outreach Loans needed to strive to gain competitive advantage, or that to gain competitive advantage Outreach Loans looked to develop new ways of doing business.

> Understanding the nature of emergence will necessarily lead to taking a different attitude to probabilistic modelling and prediction.

When Bilal, while getting into his car at a local shopping centre car park, is approached by a stranger asking 'Can you arrange a loan for me?' there is an element of surprise and emergence. It may be that, with this interaction taking place late at night in darkness and isolation (some shopping centres have all night services), Bilal thought he was about to be mugged but was surprised, instead, to find himself in a situation where there was the possibility to create new business. There remains, however, a sense in which this interaction can be seen as predictable. After all, the car has been decaled so as to invite such custom. If, following this encounter, Bilal had set up a marketing campaign in dark car parks late at night, this could be more convincingly seen as emergent behaviour.

> Understanding the principle of emergence we can take different strategies... what becomes important is developing sensitivity or receptivity to the emergent interface... to communicate our understandings with one another.

So, what are some implications of emergence for understanding organisational life? Understanding the nature of emergence will necessarily lead to taking a different attitude to probabilistic modelling and prediction. Rather than expect such modelling to offer accuracy, we can look to what else the modelling may offer, such as increasing our awareness of the assumptions brought by all of those involved in the situation.

Understanding the principle of emergence we can take different strategies. First, what becomes important is developing sensitivity or receptivity to the emergent interface. There is a need to develop our own capacities and those of others to 'read' situations, to really pay attention to what is occurring, and to communicate our understandings with one another.

Secondly, to foster sensitive and appropriate responses to novel emergences, care should be given to how prescriptively situations are managed. Where behaviours are tightly prescribed there is little capacity for improvisation. Stilted standardized behaviours at the micro-level quickly turn organisations into 'white elephant' institutions, unable to respond to rapidly changing conditions and environments.

Now, to return to the third point – that human perceptions and understandings co-arise with emergences in organisations. How can understanding this be of assistance? This perspective begs the question of what, in an organisation, is merely a new observation and what is a catalyst of change. Getting to the bottom of this dilemma is not at all helpful. It is just another case of asking 'What came first, the chicken or the egg?'. What is productive is that, while being aware of these principles of emergence, we can focus on 1) developing heightened sensitivity to indicators of emergence, and 2) seeding (fostering) emergence through sensitising conditions.

To illustrate, let us return to Wolfram's modelling of plant growth. Through our heightened sensitivity to indicators of emergence via the knowledge that it is at the tips of stems where growth occurs, we can notice possible future growth patterns. We can sensitise conditions for tree development (foster emergence) by, for example, tip pruning to encourage growth towards a more compact bushy form.

When confronted with a problem in an organisational setting, a manager could take a 'management by correction' approach: track down an apparent source or cause, then individually institute a 'solution' (which may have positive or negative effects). Or one could

> ... care should be given to how prescriptively situations are managed. .... Stilted standardized behaviours at the micro-level quickly turn organisations into 'white elephant' institutions, unable to respond to rapidly changing conditions and environments.

take a 'management through creation' approach: bring together all those involved in the situation for a discursive exploratory conversation. Doing this would allow the dynamics of the 'problem' to come forward, and would foster trust amongst the participants (presuming care and consideration of one another is part of the commitment to promoting and protecting *communicative connectedness*). This conversation provides a way of developing heightened sensitivity to any indicators of emergent potential solutions. While some people may be more naturally gifted at recognising indicators of emergence, or have schooled themselves in looking for such indicators, the conversation allows such insights to be shared, debated and further developed. Often, too, where no one is particularly practised in noting indicators, it will be through the discursive conversation that awareness develops.

Further, such conversations serve to seed or generate emergence through sensitising conditions. Involving everyone in discussing the nature of the problem and noting directions of possible future emergences is to sensitise conditions. A benefit of such involvement is the energetic engagement of those who are part of the process. The 'solution' then becomes that which the system (all who are involved) has eyes and energy for; it is a solution created through *communicative connectedness*. There are, of course, costs and benefits to such a process. Similarly, there are costs and benefits to utilising the more traditional management process of management by correction, where causal factors are linearly traced. Management by correction has the benefit of often taking less time and involving fewer people. In some situations this may be the most effective approach. However, if managers are unskilled in reading indicators of emergence, the correction may lead to devastation. The price for taking a 'management through creation' approach is that the process may carry with it the unsettling effect of bringing into awareness the constant discordant rumble (voices, opinions and concerns) of the affected. This is not to say that such unsettling dynamics would be absent with a 'management by correction' approach.

Here, though, it may be that such dynamics are deliberately ignored or are no longer clearly accessible to management. Either way ignoring such dynamics is perilous, for they too may be indicators of emergence!

2.5 Modern management theory and complexity

The complexity approach I have outlined is in radical opposition to that of modern or 'scientific' management theory. Frederick Winslow Taylor, often described as 'the father of modern management', was guided by very different principles. Taylor did not recognise the capacity of everyone to make sense for themselves and learn from their interactions. He made a distinction between *workers* as *brainless and unthinking hands* and *management* as *more intelligent*. He advocated that *all of the planning which under the old system was done by the workman, as a result of his personal experience, must of necessity under the new management system be done by management* (Taylor 1967:38). This logic remains pervasive today, informing the hierarchical image of organisations. As Clegg, Kornberger and Pitsis (2005:57) explain:

The more or less inert body (the structure) of the organisation has to have its 'hands' informed and directed (and, if necessary, corrected) by its 'head', the top management. Management develops the vision that tells the organisation where to go, the strategic intent that gives the organisation its direction... .

In contrast, a complexity approach suggests that an organisation consists of the sense-making and learning of all those involved and that its very existence is dependent upon the ongoing self-organising interactions and accommodations of all. This view sees all as co-contributors, the potentiality of all contributing to the strategic potential of the organisation. Taking relationality or conditionality as fundamental to human organisations provides a very different basis for understanding organisational functioning and emergence. This view contrasts with the idea that *an organisation without management and*

> A complexity approach suggests that an organisation consists of the sense-making and learning of all those involved and that its very existence is dependent upon the ongoing self-organising interactions and accommodations of all.

control is almost a contradiction in terms (Robbins and Barnwell 2002:19). With a complexity image, management of organisations becomes something different, the nature of which will be unpacked in the following chapters.

2.6 A complexity analysis of fractal fragment (1) Outreach Loans Bank

In this chapter, the complexity cosmography introduced depicts living systems as dynamic networks of many self-organising entities or agents (cells, individuals, communities, firms, cities, nations) constantly interacting, and reacting to each other. This perspective indicates that if there is to be any coherent behaviour in an organisation, it arises from the interactions and accommodations (competition and cooperation) among the agents themselves (as self-organising, dynamic and emergent beings). In this view, the behaviour of the whole organisation emerges from local relationships, with these resulting from the almost infinite number of moment-by-moment decisions made by all of the individual agents.

Outreach Loans Bank comprises a dynamic network of many self-organising agents. Many of these are individual people, such as Jay and Bilal and other mobile lenders, their supervising sales officer, and the particular person in head office from whom they require specific information. Other self-organising agents are groups such as the sales department, the staff who work out of head office and so on. Each person and group (team, section or department) is constantly interacting and reacting to what the other self-organising agents are doing. A complexity perspective sees the overall coherence of the behaviour of the Outreach Loans Bank, what it does, its cultures and economic successes, as arising from interactions and accommodations (competition and cooperation) among the agents themselves. In this way the behaviour of Outreach Loans Bank is understood as emergent, resulting from the moment by moment decisions and behaviour of the individual agents. This view sees the control of Outreach Loans Bank as highly dispersed and decentralized, residing within the self-organising and dynamic emergence of the agents themselves. Control through senior management, department heads or head office is reinterpreted to mean *to influence* or in the idiom of complexity, *to perturbate*, to disturb the self-organising trajectory of the individual agents such that there may be greater coherence between the self-organising emergence of individual agents and the self-organising emergence of the Bank as a whole.

> A complexity view sees both [the organisation's] past evolution and future potential as directly dependent upon multiple minute relationships and interactions.

Outreach Loans Bank is rich with potential. A complexity view sees both its past evolution and future potential as directly dependent upon multiple minute relationships and interactions. The state of the organisation that does unfold is viewed as the result of the interaction of local relationships. The overseeing and shaping of positive local relationships thus becomes a vital management function.

2.6.1 Introducing the complexity metaphor fitness landscape

While I have thus far geared my analysis of fractal fragment (1) around the complexity principles discussed above, I want to introduce the complexity metaphor of *fitness landscape* to further enliven and add depth of insight to the analysis.

The concept of *fitness landscape* emerged out of biological research being developed in the 1930s by Sewell Wright, a geneticist, who was interested in depicting how different combinations of gene variants meant that certain individuals would be better matched and do better in different circumstances (Lewin 1999). Wright used the imagery of a landscape to represent fitness probabilities, depicting these as peaks and valleys. Stuart Kaufman, theoretical biologist and prominent contributor to complexity, took the concept further in showing how for any one entity the other entities around it are its environment, and vice versa.

He gives a wonderful example, telling a story of imaginary developments generated by interactions between a fly and frog. So, let's imagine a fly:

It has a fitness landscape. Now imagine a frog. It has a fitness landscape too. But they're not independent. The frog shoots out its tongue, zap, the fly's gone. That's part of life. Now suppose the fly evolves slippery feet so that the frog's tongue doesn't stick. The frog goes without dinner, and its peak on the fitness landscape goes down: it's less fit. The fly is fitter, and so its peak rises. So the coupled landscapes change, each responding to the other. (Lewin 1999:58)

Now let us consider how the concept of fitness landscape may be employed in the organisational domain. For complex systems such as Outreach Loans Bank to survive (and thrive), there must be a certain match between what the organisation does and how it functions and its wider environment or context. In other words, its fitness landscape is critically important. Landscape refers to the sum total of the system's multiple environments or contexts. For Outreach Loans Bank this includes its social, cultural, technical, economic, political, physical context and so on. Fitness refers to the chance of survival yielded by the relationship between the entity/system and its landscape. In complex systems, small co-evolutionary matches determine fitness. There needs to be continuing coherence between the self-organising evolution of the system and its landscape. The principle behind Outreach Loans Bank (having mobile lenders operating within localities and visiting people in their homes and workplaces) is to improve the likelihood of a more positive co-evolutionary match (in simplest terms this can be depicted as being between the officers and clients/potential clients). The reason why Outreach Loans Bank is likely to result in a positive co-evolutionary outcome as opposed to a negative one (which is distinctly possible according to complexity) may be explained, again using a complexity idiom. Complexity notes that while systems may exist in various states, the state that does unfold, in this case the loan relationship, is greatly

> For complex systems... to survive (and thrive), there must be a certain match between what the organisation does and how it functions and its wider environment or context. In other words, its fitness landscape is critically important.

influenced by the interaction of local relationships. The mobile loan process is, in part, predicated on increasing awareness about local relationships and, through increased awareness and the resultant positive and improved *communicative connectedness* (between the officers and their local communities), local interactions are improved and the organisation of Outreach Loans Bank thus moves closer to a positive co-evolutionary match with its landscape.

In complex human activity systems, relationships really matter. A way of fostering relationships is through communication; communication really matters. The key, however, is that these relationships and communications are part of and sensitive to local conditions. Placing officers as mobile lenders within local communities enhances the chance of there being good communication and good relationships. However, this strategy cannot ensure this outcome. If a Loans Officer is not sensitive to the local conditions and fails to build *communicative connectedness* (good relationships through communication), the strategy may lead to undermining the Bank's reputation which may, in turn, lead to dismissal of the officer or the failure of the Bank to thrive or survive. If there is a mismatch between loans officers and their local community of potential clients, this will have implications for the larger organisation. Similarly, if *communicative connectedness* is not fostered, in terms of the internal community of the organisation, it will be detrimental to the whole organisation. If, for example, the relationship between mobile lenders and head office staff is antagonistic and results in situations where Officers are unable to effectively meet the needs of their clients, the Bank may lose business.

So, here we have two examples of the critical importance to the whole organisation of small authopoietic (self-producing and self-organising) loops. The self-organising dynamic emergence of individual agents must not be taken lightly. Rather than focus on prediction and control, the criticality to the organisation of the nature of small autopoietic loops reinforces the need to investigate and develop structural arrangements, processes and procedures that build on and enhance a climate conducive of coherence between the autopoietic processes of individuals, teams, sections, divisions and the whole organisation.

Complexity, in common with other disciplines and areas of study, constitutes a contested discourse. Complexity can be thought of as both a paradigm and an emerging contested discourse. It constitutes a paradigm in that it presents a particular way of seeing, a means of discerning pattern and order via certain habits of thought, and a distinctive collection of ideas, concepts and language. It constitutes a contested discourse in that as people thoughtfully engage, they refine and build on the ideas, developing nuances that relate to their own histories of being, interests and range of contexts.

In concluding this chapter, I want to indicate something of the richness of the contested discourse concerned with studying and working with organisations from a complexity perspective. As my aim in this book is to introduce complexity in an accessible way to people interested in organisations, I have tried to leave out the more obscure and write about that which can be communicated most clearly. In doing this, I have left out much of the contestation of the discourse. To remedy this (at least a little), I include here a sample of my sources and related publications for those interested in expanding their engagement. The list is meant to suggest directions in which your imagination can travel according to its own interests.

Further reading

Basic complexity concepts

Ashby, W. (1962) 'Principles of the self-organising system', *Principles of self-organisation: Transactions of the University of Illinois Symposium.* H. Von Foerster and G. Zopf Jr. (eds.) London: Pergamon Press.

Complex adaptive systems (http://en.wikipedia.org/wiki/Complex_ adaptive_system#cite_note-0)

Hodgson. G. (2000) 'The concept of emergence in social science: Its history and importance', *Emergence.* 2(4), 65-77.

Johnson, S. (2001) *Emergence.* Ringwood, Vic.: Penguin.

Kauffman, S. (1995) *At home in the universe: The search for the laws of self-organisation and complexity.* Oxford: Oxford University Press.

Lewin, R. (1999) *Complexity: Life at the edge of chaos.* Chicago: University of Chicago Press.

Waldrop, M. (1992) *Complexity.* New York: Simon and Schuster.

Wolfram, S. (2002) *A new kind of science.* Champaign, IL: Wolfram Media.

Complexity and organisations

Baets, W. (2006) *Complexity, learning and organisations.* London: Routledge.

Lissack, M. (1999) 'Complexity: the science, its vocabulary, and its relation to organisations', *Emergence.* 1(1)110-126.

Mitleton-Kelly, E. (2006) 'Co-evolutionary integration: the co-creation of a new organisational form following a merger and acquisition', *Emergence: Complexity and Organisation* 8:2:36-47.

Mitleton-Kelly, E. (2006 'A complexity approach to co-creating an innovative environment', *World Futures.* 62:223-239.

About organisations

Clegg, S., Kornberger, M. and Pitsis, T. (2005) *Managing and organisations.* London: Sage.

Grey, C. (2005) *A very short, fairly interesting and reasonably cheap book about studying organizations.* London: Sage.

Robbins, S. and Barnwell, N. (2002) *Organisation Theory: Concepts and cases.* Frenchs Forest: Prentice Hall, Pearson Education Australia.

Taylor, F. (1967) *Principles of scientific management.* New York: Harper.

Philosophically interesting

Dillon, M. (2000) 'Poststructuralism, complexity and poetics', *Theory, Culture & Society* 17(5):1-26.

3. COMPLEXITY PHRASE SPACE

3.1 Metaphors and concepts in sense making

So far the focus has been on introducing the basic organising principles or habits of thought that characterise a complexity perspective, with one exception. In concluding my analysis of Outreach Loans Bank, *fitness landscape* was introduced as a metaphor for describing the relationship between an organisation and its multiple contexts. This chapter continues the process of introducing the phraseology or *phrase space* of complexity by presenting specific complexity concepts as metaphors to provide thought-provoking and productive ways of understanding organisational forms, processes and practices.

In my presentation of complexity metaphors I have three aims: first, to assist you in becoming familiar with a range of specific complexity metaphors; secondly, to illustrate how these can be utilised in exploring and reinterpreting major organisational concepts; and thirdly, I want to demonstrate how you may utilise complexity to develop your own original insights about organisation-related issues. It is this third aim that has the most lasting value and is of the greatest importance. The capacity to generate your own complexity-based insights signifies that you are engaging in *complexity mediational means*, utilising complexity habits of thought in your sense-making processes. To utilise complexity mediational means is to actively work with the view offered by a complexity lens. Here you will find no pre-set answers. Here you enter the realm of considered thoughtfulness, where the challenge is to imaginatively apply the complexity metaphors in ways that you judge as authentic and productive.

You will find that I tend to blur together the ideas of concept and metaphor. This is because I see all concepts as metaphorical in nature. Our concepts – thoughts, ideas, notions or theoretical constructs – are intimately related to our consciousness, to the lens via which we 'see' the world of our experience. Hence, our concepts create for us certain ways of structuring experience. Metaphor implies the creation of an idea or symbol, through applying a term or phrase literally to something to which it is not literally applicable. In a sense we think metaphorically all of the time, as we only ever 'see' the world of experience via our concepts. In making a metaphorical comparison we do more than just create an analogy, we create new qualities of connection, new relationships and, finally, the framework that creates the meaning that our experiences have for us. In his carefully argued and thoughtful book *Physics as Metaphor* (1983), Roger Jones shows how even the most fundamental concepts of physics – space, time, matter and number – are, essentially, intimately *related to consciousness and are guaranteed of no objective, external status by physics* and thus would be better thought of as metaphorical, in that they *represent a part of the human experience (the so-called physical world) which breathes life and value into that experience and creates the meaning which that experience has for us* (Jones 1983:51).

> In making a metaphorical comparison we do more than just create an analogy, we create new qualities of connection, new relationships and, finally, the framework that creates the meaning that our experiences have for us.

3.2 *Fractal fragment (3) Ryan, Liverpool Catholic Club*

As each metaphor is introduced, I show how it can be used to generate new and productive interpretations of what is involved in 'how organisations get things done'. I will be drawing on the work of one of my students, Ryan Gould, who undertook a complexity-informed inquiry into the Liverpool Catholic Club (LCC) for his Honours research project (Gould 2007).

I asked Ryan to provide an introduction, depicting some of the background and history of the LCC. He explained:

'The LCC evolved from a social game of golf amongst 24 friends to an influential and highly respected registered Club. One Sunday afternoon each month, the All Saints Golf Club, all members of the local

parish (including priests and volunteers), enjoyed a social game of golf after they had finished their Sunday duties. The comment was often made by the event organisers that, "We should finish the game and be able to go back to our own club for a drink". It was this desire that gave rise to the LCC, which was officially opened and blessed on December 1st, 1979, some 10 years later.'

'Just as the organisers of the All Saints Golf Club provided refreshments for the thirsty golfers, the modern LCC provides its members and their guests with discounted refreshments in a calm and harmonic social atmosphere. Beginning with just one fulltime employee, the Club now employs a staff of approximately three hundred.'

The LCC is one of a number of registered Clubs, each established by a community interested in supporting a common purpose. The LCC, as with other Catholic Clubs, supports education and other activities of the Catholic community as well as making a contribution to the wider community (by providing, for example, community development funds and facilities for a range of local groups).

As part of the research project, Ryan conducted a series of interviews with various senior managers as well as frontline staff responsible for the catering and gaming divisions of the LCC, which, as he says, *'generated findings about the LCC way'*. He goes on to explain:

'I think this is best understood from two perspectives. The first describes the way in which the LCC has recruited and developed its staff, while the second describes how such a recruitment program has led to the way in which the LCC staff get things done.'

'In the early years most employees were members who were seeking to supplement their family income through casual and part-time employment at the Club. This practice continues, with most staff being brought in along family lines. As one of my interviewees stated: "The club is mostly, 80%, all family. Somebody knows somebody...They look after each other".'

Ryan considers that this recruitment style has supported the sense among employees of a distinctive LCC way *'because the people recruited already have knowledge and respect for the processes that lead to the provision of quality services offered by the LCC'*.

'Another factor,' he went on to say, *'is that many employees move around, taking different positions. Most have experience in working in a number of sections, such as catering (snack shop, coffee shop, garden restaurant, family restaurant, bistro and function centre) and house (reception, bar, KENO, TAB, slot machines and so on). Seeing themselves as the LCC family, staff say they are able to change positions as required and this ensures the smooth running and efficiency of the Club.'*

Having introduced the background and history of the LCC, I will continue to develop this fractal fragment (3) and tell you more about the LCC as I introduce and explain each of the complexity metaphors below.

3.3 Complexity metaphors

The complexity metaphors introduced here, together with *fitness landscape*, are those that I have found most useful in understanding organisational life. Each metaphor is introduced and described with reference to fractal fragment (3). An illustrative analytical description of fractal fragment (3) concludes the chapter, showing how working with the metaphors may generate productive new insights and understandings.

The complexity metaphors introduced are:
1. Phase space – phrase space
2. Communicative connectedness
3. Sensitive dependence on initial conditions
4. Edge of chaos – chaotic edge
5. Attractors
6. Fractality.

3. COMPLEXITY PHRASE SPACE

3.3.1 Phase space – phrase space

Phase space is, in essence, an imaginary multi-dimensional space, a mathematical construct in which numbers are turned into pictures, where we can 'see' the movement of a complex dynamic entity over time. *Phase space* describes the space comprising all the possible states of a complex entity. Thus, in a *phase space* we can see plotted regions of stability and instability and can trace the entity's entire evolution. What is particularly interesting is that *phase space* shows us that, although there are a great many possibilities, an entity occupies only a minute proportion of its possible *phase space*. So, for example, H_2O may exist as air, (a gaseous state), water (a liquid state) or ice (a solid state) with each state a function of pressure, temperature and composition.

Phrase space takes this concept and applies it to human beings and notes that, although it is possible to make sense of life in a great many ways and hold a great many different theories and beliefs, we too live within a minute proportion of possibilities, as individuals and as societies (Kuhn, Woog and Hodgson 2003, Kuhn and Woog 2007). The idea of *phrase space* is beautifully depicted by the great German poet Rainer Maria Rilke in his *Letters to a Young Poet* when he writes: *For if we think of this existence of the individual as a larger or smaller room, it appears that most people learn to know only a corner of their room, a place by the window, a strip of floor on which they walk up and down.* (Rilke 2004:51)

Playing on the word 'phrase', *phrase space* is used to describe the way that our ideas and, consequently, our ways of living are mediated through language. Chilean neurobiologists Humberto Maturana and Francisco Varela and, similarly, philosophers, psychologists and sociologists (such as Wittgenstein, Rorty, Kelly, and Vickers) stress the importance of language to consciousness itself:

Consciousness and mind belong to the realm of social couplings. Moreover, since we exist in language, the domains of discourse that we generate become part

> ... *phase space* shows us that, although there are a great many possibilities, an entity occupies only a minute proportion of its possible *phase space*.

> *Phrase space* takes this concept and applies it to human beings and notes that... we too live within a minute proportion of possibilities, as individuals and as societies

of our domain of existence and constitute part of the environment in which we conserve identity and adaptation. (Maturana and Varela 1987:234)

The 'space' we each live within is strongly shaped by the communities of which we are a part. Being part of Mongol society, throat singing is normal. For a twenty-first century American, Australian or European person, throat singing is alien (but may be fascinating). As a member of the July 2008 US Geographical Survey, you would probably consider the area north of the Arctic Circle as constituting one of the last remaining prospective areas for petroleum mining. As a member of the Shell Oil Company, you would likely think that oil production is a noble occupation contributing to the health and well being of society and see no threat to the environment by taking new leases in the Chukchi Sea in northwest Alaska. As a member of the World Wildlife Fund, however, you may consider these new leases as environmentally dangerous and the very source of problems in the Arctic and beyond, threatening the future health and well being of humanity. In each case, our group allegiance or social coupling reveals and shapes understanding.

> Taking organisation studies as a whole, I could posit that its movements in *phrase space* are a function of changes in pre-occupation and reflect certain popularised views about how best to motivate large groups of people to get things done... .

As with H_2O, where periods of stability/instability can be viewed as a function of pressure, temperature and composition, we can inquire into and seek to separate out the major influences of which a *phrase space* is a function. Taking organisation studies as a whole, I could posit that its movements in *phrase space* are a function of changes in preoccupation and reflect certain popularised views about how best to motivate large groups of people to get things done, such as via the scientific management of Taylorism (Frederick Winslow Taylor's carrot and stick approach, seeing people as motivated by pleasure and pain) or bureaucratic structural arrangements. A longitudinal reading of the interactions shown in Figure 2 in Chapter 1 would show something of this organisational *phrase space* (limited however, by the dimensions I have taken into account) over time (from the time of the early Greeks to the 21st century). Or I could take, as an example, a particular organisation's processes,

3. COMPLEXITY PHRASE SPACE

such as the moving assembly lines of the Ford motor company in the 1920s and 1930s. Undertaking a *phrase space* analysis, I may describe these processes as a function of the dominance of certain theories about organising (scientific management, Taylorism and bureaucratic processes), together with other factors, such as cultural norms, religious beliefs, employment levels and economic needs.

It is interesting that we can become aware of our position in *phrase space*, aware of the social couplings or conversations that shape our ideas, aware of how our views align with or differ from those of others. What is even more interesting is that we can describe our position and, in so doing, build increased understanding of the contextual interrelatedness of our positioning. Through our ability to discuss and describe, we can talk our position into being. We can even talk into being our preferred position. It is in relation to this capacity to discuss and describe, to talk into being, that my colleagues and I have found the complexity metaphor *phrase space* to be of particular use in coming to terms with organisation practices.

We can pay attention to *phrase space* to help us to understand the way that organisations generate their specific organisational dynamics whilst evolving in ongoing contextual coupling within their environments (maintaining their fitness landscape). Ryan indicated something of the *phrase space* characterising the LCC when he reported that the floor staff of the LCC refer to their Duty Managers as 'white shirts'. Ryan noted how the use of this affectionate and informal title serves to demarcate 'who is truly one of us' (an employee/member of the LCC), thus contributing to a sense of community amongst Club employees. Using such a colloquial term also fits well with the Club's landscape, described demographically as predominantly working-class.

Parallelling *phase space*, we find that people too may move quickly from having the potential for an infinite range of possible states to occupying a limited space, through communicating experiences

> *Phrase space* shapes not only our social environments but also our sense of who we are.

and interpretations such that a communal, sectoral or organisational perspective emerges. *Phrase space* shapes not only our social environments but also our sense of who we are. This idea has been well recognised by philosophers, neurobiologists and psychologists alike. Narrative therapy, for example, is designed to assist people in telling different narratives about themselves and their lives in order for them to become different and to live differently.

Organisational theorists, in giving considerable attention to using narrative approaches in organisational research (see Boje 2001 for example), or in promoting the benefits of purposefully using storytelling as a technique for influencing organisational emergence (see Denning 2000, Weick 1995 or the *Journal of Storytelling and Business Excellence*), implicitly recognise the importance of *phrase space*.

As with narrative therapy, approaches to story telling in organisations are based on understanding that changing organisational narratives means changing organisational procedures and practices. Robinson (1981:60), for example, argues that *telling stories about remarkable experiences is one of the ways in which people try to make the unexpected expectable, hence manageable.*

> *Although ideas are formed in the minds of individuals, interaction between individuals typically plays a critical role... communities of interaction contribute to the amplification and development of new knowledge.*
> (Nonaka 2004:166)

Ideas relating to *phrase space*, in terms of the prescribing influence of group membership on what is known and valued and on how things get done, have been recognised in organisation studies literature. Wenger's focus on 'communities of practice' (Wenger 2004) brings attention to organisational *phrase space* by emphasising the impact of social dynamics on how organisations get things done. Nonaka's (2004) spiral theory of organisational knowledge creation inherently recognises humans as self-organising, dynamic and emergent and organisational knowing as being created through ongoing interactions between individuals and their organisational context:

Although ideas are formed in the minds of individuals, interaction between individuals typically plays a critical role in developing these ideas. That is to say, communities of interaction contribute to the amplification and development of new knowledge. (Nonaka 2004:166)

As a metaphor to aid understanding, *phrase space* is important because it serves as both a revelation and a means of description. It is a revelation in that it reveals multiple processes of self-organisation, dynamics and emergence in social situations, such as those constituted within organisational processes and activities. Complex systems are by nature complex and therefore difficult to describe. *Phrase space* is an effective means of describing a complex system to an observer.

In particular, for organisation practitioners, *phrase space* provides:

1. Greater emphasis on the realm of possibility by drawing attention to the realisation that ways of knowing and doing represent limited, habitual and socially supported frameworks within a space of infinite possibility.
2. A reminder that paying attention to the *phrase space* will yield important information about the attitudes, aspirations, criticisms and knowledge of the participants (or community of practice) which is crucial to working towards creating optimal conditions and circumstances for the future prosperity/ sustainability of the organisation.
3. A framework for recognising the importance of presenting qualities of relationship, or *communicative connectedness* for future organisational emergence.

3.3.2 *Communicative connectedness*

My colleague Robert Woog created the term *communicative connectedness* (Woog 2004) as a short hand way of describing the quality of interconnectedness between people. From a complexity perspective, because everything, whether tightly or loosely coupled, is understood as being

> From a complexity perspective, because everything, whether tightly or loosely coupled, is understood as being related to everything else, the nature and quality of interconnections is critical.

related to everything else, the nature and quality of interconnections is critical. Remember the story of slime mould from Chapter 2? Although each cell of *Dictyostelium discordeum* self-organises, it is through local connections that macro behaviour emerges. In a similar manner, the existence of human activity systems and the ways by which they change are dependent upon how the people involved connect with one another. However, there is a huge difference between slime mould and people. When the chemical change signals dispersal or aggregation, individual slime mould cells do not respond with 'But I don't like linking to …' or 'I don't feel like doing that just now' and so on. If you are slime mould, you do not have to worry about presenting yourself as trustworthy, or decide how to determine if those around you are worthy of trust. *Communicative connectedness* between people implicates all aspects of the human as a psycho-socio-ecological being.

In all that we do, our relationships with other people really matter and are dependent upon the nature and quality of our communication with one another. Conversation forms the primary means of communicative interaction. The types and quality of communication between all of the people involved, both within and external to the organisation, shape the nature of the organisation. Organisations can, in this way, be seen as existing through conversations, shaped by the *communicative connectedness* of all participants. Patricia Shaw makes this point when she says that she prefers to write about *conversing as organising* and *organising as conversing,* than to write of conversations as taking place in organisations (Shaw 2002:11).

> Organisations can... be seen as existing through conversations, shaped by the *communicative connectedness* of all participants.

Conversational interactions are clearly not uniform between all people but are influenced by a great many factors, such as personality, past experiences, cultural norms, and the presenting context and setting and the interpretations of it. According to 'systemic functional linguistics' (concerned with analysing communication from a holistic perspective), conversation always takes place within a communicative context and setting, and these determine the words we choose and how we

3. COMPLEXITY PHRASE SPACE

say them. So how we converse varies with the person to whom we are speaking (a colleague, subordinate, the boss), the purpose of the exchange (requesting information, giving orders, apologising) and the mode (email, phone, face to face) and so on.

It is evident that there are a great many things going on at once. The relationships we have with the people we talk to are critical to the unfolding quality of the conversation. On the one hand, conversational interactions are influenced by the *type* of relationship we have (parent, boss, shop assistant, supervisee etc.), and on the other hand, the *quality* of the relationship (trusting, one where I can share a joke, one where I feel on edge).

> *Communicative connectedness* shapes shared assumptions about work practices and ensures that members share the standards and purposes characteristic of that practice...

Through *communicative connectedness*, humans bring about sophisticated forms of joint action. *Communicative connectedness* shapes shared assumptions about work practices and ensures that members share the standards and purposes characteristic of that practice, thus enabling those involved to more easily present themselves and read others as truthful and worthy of trust. *Communicative connectedness* also shapes future practice. As Stacey, Griffin and Shaw (2000) note, it is through micro interactions that people perpetually reconstruct the future.

Communicative connectedness can be thought of as a conscious or adaptive response to felt uncertainty. In many different ways people show awareness of the role of *communicative connectedness* in helping them cope with the unfolding nature of complex dynamic systems. In the context of organisations as firms, a number of stylised forms of fostering and maintaining *communicative connectedness* are apparent. In terms of formal activities there are planning meetings, symposia, conferences, workshops and so on. Casual or semi-formal equivalents, where communication carries the vestment of gossip, include water cooler conversations, corridor conversations and semi-structured social gatherings such as 'Friday night happy hour', various games of sport, BBQs and so on. The major difference between the formal and informal styles concerns validity and reliability of the information exchanged and developed. In formal activities, the validity of the *communicative connectedness* is defined and safeguarded by the very formality of the process. With informal activities, validity and reliability are established through consensual agreement.

Fractal fragment (3) demonstrates the significance of *communicative connectedness*. Ryan describes the Club as *a self-organising network of communities operating within dynamic, emergent and somewhat chaotic environments*. These communities, which he labels as 'house' (primarily relating to those staff working in reception, the bar and slot machine area), 'catering' (comprising mostly staff of the various restaurants, bistros and coffee shops) and 'other' (mostly staff of the sporting complex and cemetery), were shown to be each characterised by strong *communicative connectedness*. Importantly, there was also an overall sense of *communicative connectedness* between Club employees and the whole of the LCC. This was seen to be due to a number of factors, notably the history of the Club, with employees traditionally sourced from members of the families involved in the LCC, and the common experience of staff coming up through the ranks of employment in the Club and thereby belonging to more than one of the communities. His research revealed, however, that there was a disjuncture between *floor staff* and *upstairs* (senior management). Participants in his project (floor staff) were concerned about this lack of relationship and requested '*improved communication between upstairs and floor staff*'. Interestingly, the quality of *communicative connectedness* between Ryan and the research participants was also found to be critical to the validity of his inquiry project. As Ryan reflected:

While my work colleagues and I shared a drink after the coherent conversations sessions, many of them spoke about how our friendships had allowed them to speak honestly about their organisation without any fear of consequence. Our pre-existing relationships had increased trust and cohesion. From a researcher's perspective, it also meant that I had a profound understanding of the 'local tongue', the language and behaviours of the LCC. (Gould 2007:59)

In organisational contexts, *communicative connectedness* may be developed in a number of ways. Managers sensitised to the importance of *communicative connectedness* can seek to foster relationships of greater quality, by putting structures and practices in place that facilitate information exchanges or that enable people to develop respectful, trusting relationships. Strategies that promote *open-ended, exploratory conversation amongst attentive, engaged humans* (Shaw 2002:162) are designed to facilitate strength and resilience of *communicative connectedness*.

> The nature and quality of *communicative connectedness* can be used as an indicator of the health or robustness of an organisation.

The nature and quality of *communicative connectedness* can be used as an indicator of the health or robustness of an organisation. By tracing movements and rises and falls in *communicative connectedness* it is possible to understand why certain problems arise. An analysis of the nature and quality of *communicative connectedness* can provide much productive information about patterns that connect – be these within or outside the organisation.

3.3.3   Sensitive dependence on initial conditions

The third complexity metaphor, *sensitive dependence on initial conditions* often referred to as *the butterfly effect,* stresses the significant influence of the *initial conditions* and small perturbations on shaping the overall emergence of a complex system. This metaphor originates from research into weather patterns. In 1961, mathematician and meteorologist Edward Lorenz discovered that just one small change to the set of numbers he typed into his weather-producing computer program – he rounded off .506127 to .506 – caused his computer weather system to produce patterns that grew further and further apart. He was surprised to find that a difference of only one part in a thousand resulted in a great difference in predictable weather patterns. His findings challenged a long-standing philosophical assumption basic to science: that *given an approximate knowledge of a system's initial conditions and an understanding of natural law, one can calculate the approximate behaviour of the system.* (Gleick1990:15)

Interestingly, this understanding, that small inputs can have dramatically disproportionate consequences and that slight differences in *initial conditions* can produce very different outcomes, has long been recognised informally in every day life and is illustrated by this well known saying:

For want of a nail, the shoe was lost.
For want of a shoe, the horse was lost.
For want of a horse, the rider was lost.
For want of a rider the message was lost.
For want of a message, the battle was lost.
For want of a battle, the kingdom was lost.
All for want of a nail.

Had we been familiar with the complexity metaphor *sensitive dependence on initial conditions*, would we have been able to save the kingdom? I think not. At a micro level, we can know everything about nails and shoe mending and yet remain unable to predict the loss of a kingdom. The loss of the kingdom represents an emergent outcome that was highly dependent on multiple sets of *initial conditions*.

How is *sensitive dependence on initial conditions* demonstrated in fractal fragment (3)? Consider the beginning of the Liverpool Catholic Club. It is significant that it evolved from a group of priests and other members of the local Catholic parish enjoying a game of golf on a Sunday afternoon and wishing they had their own club to retire to following the game (Gould 2007). The LCC to this day is distinctly a Catholic club, embodying the usual club aims of providing cultural and sporting facilities for members and their guests, together with close links with the Catholic Church (it was officially blessed upon its opening and much of its profits directly contribute to the needs of local Catholic parishioners and related charitable causes). While my example here draws on the LCC's commonly told narrative about its own beginnings, there are other points along its history that could likewise be perceived as constituting *initial conditions*. For example, in many countries, there has recently been new legislation banning smoking from public premises such as restaurants, pubs and clubs. We can take the time at which this legislation was enacted as constituting another set of *initial conditions*, and note the continuing influence on the club of its history as a place where smoking was once an acceptable social occupation.

So, in utilising this metaphor of *sensitive dependence on initial conditions*, we need to ask, in particular organisational settings, what constitutes the *initial conditions*? Here you will need to be thoughtfully discerning. Life is made up of instances, one instance plus the next instance and so on. You will need to take into account something of the history of the phenomenon in deciding what should be focussed upon as the *initial conditions*. Is it when the company was first discussed over a BBQ amongst mates? Is it the first meeting of the new management team following a restructure? What is important is to take the presenting circumstances of concern as your starting point and then track back into the history of this situation, as therein will lie the clues to why things have emerged in the way that they have.

> What is important is to take the presenting circumstances of concern as your starting point and then track back into the history of this situation, as therein will lie the clues to why things have emerged in the way that they have.

Let me give a simple example. I am presenting at a professional conference and I introduce complexity with a demonstration using a glass of water placed towards the centre of a table. I tell the audience that the glass of water is at equilibrium when it is sitting still. I then push it towards the edge of the table. As the glass moves closer to the edge, the audience is immediately more interested. I might even tip it over, demonstrating how a new arrangement will spontaneously form – through self-organising dynamic processes. The *initial conditions* of this presentation matter enormously. It is critically important to the way that the audience reacts that I am on the podium giving a formal presentation at a conference. This being the *initial conditions* sets the manner of the audience's engagement with my demonstration. If the situation were different, such as a private meeting where your new computer is immediately below my tipping glass, then the engagement would be different.

3.3.4 Edge of chaos – chaotic edge

The *edge of chaos* represents a dynamic area within a complex entity's *phase space*. As explained in Chapter 1, the *edge of chaos* describes a far-from-equilibrium zone between order and disorder. Also described as a critical state, the *edge of chaos* is where complex self-organising systems or entities tend naturally to gravitate (Lewin 1999, Bak and Chen 1991, Packard 1988, Langton 1986).

> ... the *edge of chaos*, from the perspective of a complexity framework, is where... processes of organisational adjustment, adaptation and development are most supported and fostered.

Although it may not sound like an inviting place to be, the *edge of chaos*, from the perspective of a complexity framework, is where organisations, as complex adaptive entities, are most profitably placed. For it is here that processes of organisational adjustment, adaptation and development are most supported and fostered. However, given people's capacity for judgement and reflection, not every one sees this as a desirable location. In our research with organisations, my colleagues and I have found it useful to differentiate an *edge of chaos* attitude from what we term *chaotic edge* thinking (Kuhn, Woog and Hodgson 2003). We use the term *chaotic edge* to describe where people think of themselves and their situation as being full of threat, rather than full of potential. Have you ever tried to walk along a log? If it is on the ground, no doubt you will find it relatively easy to place your feet one after the other onto the log. But if it spans a fast running stream, you may find your sure-footedness lacking. Why? Not because the task is in itself any more difficult but purely because of your anxiety about falling off. *Chaotic edge* thinking is 'fear of falling off' thinking. It causes people to respond radically to situations.

> *Chaotic edge* thinking is 'fear of falling off' thinking. It causes people to respond radically to situations.

Edge of chaos thinking has organisations handling change effectively and developing new strategic directions as they flexibly encounter new situations and opportunities. *Chaotic edge* thinking has

Edge of chaos thinking has organisations handling change effectively and developing new strategic directions as they flexibly encounter new situations and opportunities.

organisations perceiving themselves as being under threat from almost any change or perturbation and behaving in ways designed to minimise the threat of catastrophe. Often this means a retreat to rules-based behaviour, to true and tested strategies, rather than willingness to experiment.

Returning to fractal fragment (3), it is interesting to observe responses of members of the Liverpool Catholic Club to the recent introduction of legislation prohibiting smoking inside public venues, such as restaurants, pubs and clubs. While some have taken a *chaotic edge* view, seeing the banning of smoking as spelling future doom for the Club, others manoeuvre with the times. An outdoor shelter has now been constructed with access to club amenities where people wishing to smoke may do so. Of course, paying attention to the wider community *phrase space*, it is clear that, overall, people are now more seriously concerned about the harmful effects of smoking (both active and passive). For many, to continue to allow indoor smoking in public places is to deliberately engage in risky behaviour, placing ourselves just too close to the *edge of chaos* in terms of personal health.

3.3.5 *Attractors*

Holding complex entities in particular patterns, *attractors* may be understood as energies that motivate.

Attractors function as organising forces that guide behaviour. Holding complex entities in particular patterns, *attractors* may be understood as energies that motivate. The sun functions as an *attractor* for our solar system, holding the movements and special arrangements of the planets within the system. Desire to make a profit acts as an *attractor* in shaping money movements in the stock exchange, as does depicting your behaviours as within the legal guidelines.

People may be under the influence of certain *attractors* for prolonged periods of their lives. One of the most obvious examples is the *attractor* around which a working life is organised. Consider, for example, the nature of the *attractor* or *attractor* set guiding the working lives of artists, musicians, scientists, lawyers, jockeys or bank robbers.

Even in the most chaotic situation there emerge organising principles, which on careful examination reveal a pattern and hence a shape. Politics, religion, economics and environmentalism may all act as *attractors* in a social phenomenon's dynamics. We can see this played out in the lives of individuals (such as causing someone to protest a certain development) as much as within the socio-political life of a nation (such as in the specifics of environmental planning laws, or the manner by which a country participates in international environmental forums).

People may move from being organised around one *attractor* to being organised around another. An historical example of such a shift is the movement in the Soviet Union from socialism to capitalism. Highly chaotic dynamics, commonly associated with divergence, and the decline in influence of one *attractor* with the formation of a new *attractor* were evident. The senescence of the old *attractor* and the formation of the new took place in an environment of intensely chaotic dynamics. Similarly, a time of agitation and high energy can be observed when an individual or organisation is in the process of seeking new ways of being or direction. As this is often an unconscious process, awareness of the characteristics associated with potential movement from one *attractor* to another can help those involved to understand more about their situation.

Understanding *attractors* is critically important for organisations. Getting it wrong often spells failure, from loss of a positive working culture to loss of market share. *Attractors* can operate as organising forces in multiple ways in organisations. Take, for example, personal motivations guiding work choices and behaviours. Here it is interesting to reflect on recent research into the most significant workplace *attractors* for Generation Y (people born between 1980 and 1994). Peter Sheahan (2006) in his book *Generation Y: thriving and surviving with generation Y at work* points out nine aspects of the mindset of Generation Yers, describing them as street smart,

> ... a time of agitation and high energy can be observed when an individual or organisation is in the process of seeking new ways of being or direction.

3. COMPLEXITY PHRASE SPACE

aware, lifestyle centred, independently dependent, informal, technically savvy, stimulus junkies, sceptical and impatient. Sheahan argues that Generation Yers are talented, and that to build a Generation Y-friendly organisation is to build a talent-friendly organisation. To do this it is necessary to have insight into the major *attractors* guiding Generation Y workplace choices and behaviours. Given the characteristics of Generation Y, Sheahan outlines what they want from a workplace, boss and job. For example, he says Generation Y are looking for a sense of purpose and meaning, responsibility, promotional opportunity, new challenges and experiences, fair compensation, increased employability, opportunity to express their individuality and creativity, flexibility, ethical practices, fun, a feeling of belonging and being engaged, modern and edgy, up-to-date work places and operations, and fuel to feed their passionate and optimistic outlook on life. To be aware of and to understand these *attractors* enables managers to constructively review work practices. It may well be that through the appropriate revision of procedures and processes the organisation will not lose young, enterprising and fast learning employees to competitors.

> To be aware of and to understand these *attractors* enables managers to constructively review work practices.

Let us now focus on *attractors* in the Liverpool Catholic Club. Ryan identified two powerful *attractors* guiding the self-organising emergence of the LCC. These were the family and the business. He found that family membership was the basis for people's employment in the Club. It was through the families involved that new staff were recruited. As one of his interviewees reflected: '*This club is mostly, 80%, family... They look after each other.*' Family membership also served to ensure that people behaved respectfully. For instance, when one young man began employment with the LCC his mother told him: '*Don't you embarrass your father and I... It's not just you working here you know. It's us. Our name is on display.*' In conjunction with the family, the other major *attractor* guiding the organisational behaviour and self-organising emergence of the LCC is the understanding that it is primarily a business, and needs to be managed efficiently, professionally and profitably.

In summary, paying attention to *attractors* helps an observer understand the range of organisational behaviours. If you appreciate what the *attractors* are that are driving behaviours, then you can understand how these behaviours are valid for those involved. Without identification of *attractors*, the behaviours of others may appear as irrational and illegitimate. We might ask 'How can that possibly be? Why would she or he ever choose to do that?' However, when it is apparent what the *attractors* are, we can see the behaviours of others as valid and sensible from their perspective.

3.3.6 Fractality

Simply stated, a *fractal* is an entity with characteristics simultaneously apparent across multiple scales of focus. For those familiar with complexity, *fractality* may seem like common sense. However, if you are not used to thinking fractally, the concept probably requires quite some unpacking! So let me introduce the originator of *fractality*, Benoit Mandelbrot.

Mathematical physicist, Mandelbrot, developed a new geometry of nature to describe a family of naturally occurring irregular shapes where the degree of irregularity or fragmentation is identical at all scales. Mandelbrot describes his fractal geometry as better enabling scientists *to take the measure of the universe* (1977 C1) because it provides a way of measuring certain naturally occurring 'wiggles' (such as coastlines, river systems and trees). In so doing he saw his work as solving intransigent difficulties resisting accurate measurement. As he says:

Scientists will (I am sure) be surprised and delighted to find that not a few shapes they had to call grainy, hydralike, in between, pimply, pocky, ramified, seaweedy, strange, tangled tortuous, wiggly, wispy, wrinkled, and the like, can henceforth be approached in rigorous and vigorous quantitative fashion.
(op. cit. 5)

3. COMPLEXITY PHRASE SPACE

... a *fractal* is an entity with characteristics simultaneously apparent across multiple scales of focus.

The term fractal is thus used to describe entities and systems with fractal dimensionality: having look-alike features and characteristics simultaneously apparent at different scales of focus. What is most interesting about fractals is that because of these look-alike or self-similar features, a fractal object looks the same from close up as it does from far away. Its self-similarity means that sub-systems or small sections of the fractal entity are equivalent to the whole.

Mandelbrot discovered that river systems, coastlines, trees, mountain ranges and other natural systems depict fractal dimensions and that they can be described using complicated formulas and mathematical definitions. I find it amazing that in river systems, *degrees of irregularity of local wiggles of the banks and of enormously global bends turn out to be identical* (op. cit. 111), or that all rivers and their basins are mutually similar with the ratio between a river's length and the area of its drainage basin remaining constant for all rivers. Similarly, while we may not be familiar with his mathematics, we can see *fractality* in the repeating patterns in the branching of a river or tree. See overleaf for depictions of *fractality*. We can think of *fractality* conceptually, such as in terms of the similarity between a large flowing river and the smallest stream, seeing self-similarity (or fractals) in the movement of water between earth masses at all scales, be these mountain ranges or tiny cracks in a clay pan. Looking at a photo of a fork between tree branches, we would need to see the whole tree to determine if we were looking at a forking of the trunk or of smaller branches.

Figure 3
Fractality depicted in the repeated branching of a fern

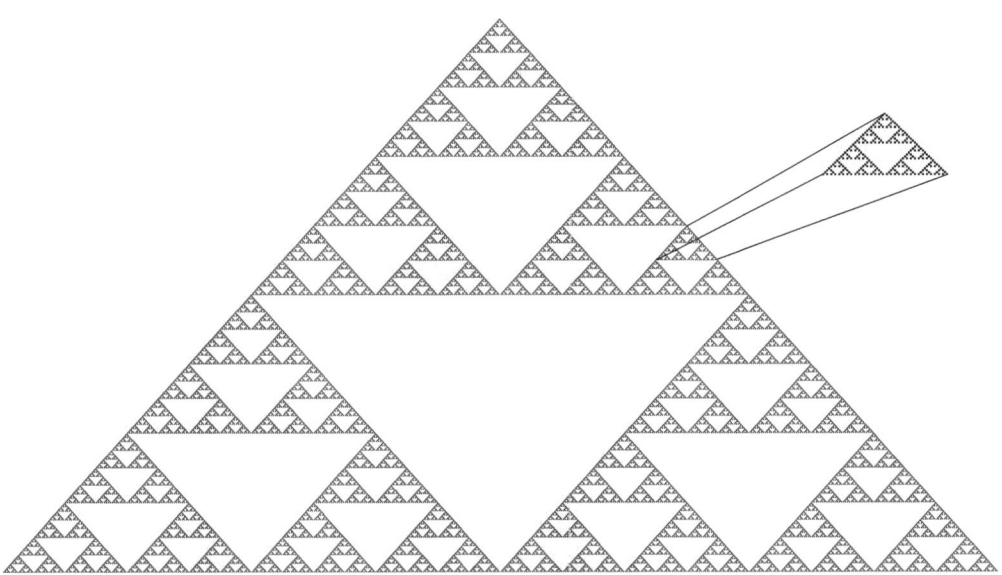

Figure 4
Fractality depicted in Stephen Wolfram's computer simulation
of repeated triangles[1]

---

1   Wolfram, S. 2002. *A new kind of science.* Champaign, IL: Wolfram Media, p. 26.
With kind permission from Stephen Wolfram, LLC. Wolframscience (www.wolfram.com)

Mandelbrot also showed that our bodies are largely made up of fractals. Our circulatory, lymph and digestive systems are each fractally organised, as are lungs, muscle tissue, small intestine and folding patterns on the brain's surface. Blood vessels, too, are fractally organised with repeated branching and similarity of functioning apparent.

It seems that others working in different time frames and within different areas of study have intuited the central idea of *fractality* – that of self-similarity across different size scales. Interestingly, Mandelbrot writes of finding comfort in many 'ancient' references as he was pursuing his own work, during *the long years when my interests were not shared by anyone, I rejoiced in discovering analogous concerns in ancient works, however fleetingly and ineffectually expressed...* (op. cit. 20). Working across physics and mathematics, it is not surprising that Mandelbrot would give examples from these areas. However, he also turns to art and shows us how great artists of the past illustrate nature in such a way as to bring us to the threshold of *fractality*.

Figure 5
The Great Wave by Katsushika Hokusai (1760-1849)

Figure 6
The Deluge by Leonardo Da Vinci (1452-1519)

The nature of *fractality* can be difficult to understand. Taking the lead from Mandelbrot's injunction that *the nature of fractals is meant to be gradually discovered by the reader, not revealed in a flash by the author* (op. cit. 5), and his own use of art to provide examples, I introduce some further descriptions that I have found helpful.

Michel de Montaigne (1533-1592) (Lopate 1995) is famous for introducing the personal essay, an informal, conversational and confessional style of writing that treats the reader like an intimate friend or companion who can understand and identify with the writer's foibles and day-to-day struggles. He thought the personal essay was a legitimate and important way of writing because of his supposition that there is a type of unity to all human experience. His statement that *every man has within himself the entire human condition*, that in writing about himself he was to some degree writing about all of us, depicts, in the language of complexity, a fractal understanding of the relationship between human beings. The kinds of self-similarity depicted by Montaigne and others writing in a personal essay style relate to certain personal pre-occupations, such as the struggle to be deeply and personally honest or to be aware of one's own ignorance or self-contradictory impulses.

3. COMPLEXITY PHRASE SPACE

Eighteenth century poet William Blake shows that he recognises the world as fractally organised when he poetically invokes fractal images in his *Auguries of Innocence*:

To see a World in a Grain of Sand
And a Heaven in a Wild Flower
Hold Infinity in the palm of your hand
And Eternity in an hour
A Robin Red breast in a Cage
Puts all heaven in a Rage…

Blake also depicts a fractal relationship between himself and a fly, beautifully describing their self-similarity in his poem *The Fly*.

Little Fly
Thy summers play,
My thoughtless hand
Has brush'd away.

Am not I
A fly like thee?
Or Art not thou
A man like me?

For I dance
And drink & sing;
Till some blind hand
Shall brush my wing.

If thought is life
And strength & breath;
And the want
Of thought is death;

Then am I
A happy fly,
If I live
Or if I die.

My favourite written evocation of *fractality* is from the field of psychology. Eminent psychologist Carl Jung describes self-similarity between the human psyche and the structure of the universe. I love the grandness and the breadth of scale:

Our psyche is set up in accord with the structure of the universe, and what happens in the macrocosm likewise happens in the infinitesimal and most subjective reaches of the psyche. (Jung 1995:368)

In a similar vein, and with typical wit, novelist Jeanette Winterson asks: *What is it you contain? The dead. Time. Light patterns of millennia exploding in your gut.* (Winterson 2005:3)

What these writers show is the power of thinking fractally. Recognition of fractal dimensions yields new insights. Thinking fractally means recognising that the global and local are embedded in all levels of social practice.

> Recognition of fractal dimensions yields new insights. Thinking fractally means recognising that the global and local are embedded in all levels of social practice.

I was surprised to see a recent television advertisement in Australia depicting such a fractal view, with its announcement that *I am, you are, we are Australia.* In the UK, this thinking is shown too by the communications company Orange in the advertising campaign *I am who I am because of everyone,* where a number of people were invited to write about their own experience of recognising how they are embedded socially. Take for example Rose Tremain's entry:

I am the ragged fur coat my English Literature teacher wore in a cold boarding school classroom
And all the stories she encouraged me to write.
I am a publisher's rejection letter
I am five publisher's rejection letters. Then six, then seven…
I am the white boots I wear in 1975 to meet the eighth publisher, Penelope Hoare
And her devastating smile of acceptance
I am Robert Merivel, and all my characters who came before and after him
I am the eyes of my readers on the underground
I am Lev, the wounded hero of The Road Home
I am Rose Tremain, winner of the Orange Broadband prize for Fiction 2008
I am all these things and all these people.
I am who I am because of everyone.

What I find even more interesting is that such fractal understanding is apparent in ancient cultures. For example, the traditional African concept of *ubuntu*, as explained by Archbishop Desmond Tutu (1999), is applied to a person who knows *that he or she belongs in a great whole and is diminished when others are humiliated or diminished, when others are tortured or oppressed.* Simply stated, this fractal understanding is evocatively expressed in the Zulu maxim *umuntu ngumuntu ngabantu – a person is a person through other persons.*

Let me now return from this foray into psychology, philosophy and the arts, to focus on the organisational context. In summary, *fractality* allows organisational settings to be examined for patterns of similarity, with the key principles being that:

- Fractals exhibit the same degree of irregularity at different scales.
- Observing a fractal you get information proportional to the scale.
- The small scale remains an equally complex microcosm of the whole.

Fractality is helpful in understanding organisational processes and potentialities. If organisations, communities, nations and so on show *fractality*, with characteristics present in the individual likewise present within larger groups (from local to global), we can choose our focus of investigation knowing that within this focus there will be information about all of the other levels. Similarly, we need to recognise that impacts, feelings and attitudes of individuals will be replicated throughout the organisation, in teams, departments, divisions, and so on. Beyond single organisations we can readily appreciate sectoral, such as financial, industrial or resource related, similarities.

Ryan's inquiry into the Liverpool Catholic Club reveals the fractal identity of the LCC and its sector. We can talk of a fractal identity when the influence of an *attractor* becomes apparent at all fractal scales. Individual, organisation and sector attitudes to the future reveal a fractal identity. At all three levels the two key *attractors* of family and business hold sway, with a concurrent move towards a more 'professional' or business orientation. Individual members/ employees, in recognising the importance of family and business both for recruitment and maintenance of the character of the LCC, consider that the LCC needs to become more business-oriented if it is to survive. As one interviewee reflected: *'I think there should be training ... the way we're growing we need proper training.'* At the level of the whole organisation, this pairing of family and business, along with greater focus on business (becoming more professional), was seen to be important to staff, from floor level to senior management, as well as to members. As one senior manager puts it: *'There were a lot of people who joined the Club who worked through the Club from barman, waiting tables to eventually become a manager. Things have changed... Education's come in to it... You now have to be qualified and skilled... the board of directors ensures that the business is run professionally... working to key indicators and percentages and profit/bottom line counts as much in the Club industry as anything.'* This fractal identity extends to the LCC's sector, the New South Wales gaming industry, with industry representatives also speaking of the need for Clubs to move from a family or community based model to that of a business model.

3.4 *Fractal fragment (4) Hanna, Lifeguard International Insurance Company*

This fractal fragment is based on conversations with Hanna who is Director of Human Relations for the South Pacific division of Lifeguard International Insurance Company.

Hanna was keen to begin her narrative about Lifeguard International Insurance Company (LIIC) by talking about how effectively her organisation used to get things done in the past, and contrasting this with the devastating impacts of new forms and processes instituted via a combined merger and radical restructure of the company. It was interesting that, towards the end of her account, Hanna reflected that although she was initially despondent about the impacts of the changes in work practices, after a period of time she saw what she called a 'tipping point', where it was evident that the new forms and processes were coming together well. She explained that from that moment of recognition, her attitude to the effects of the merger and restructure changed.

'I would say that our organisation got things done geographically up until two years ago,' she began. *'Each division, such as Scandinavian, British, North American, Central European or South Pacific, was run by an executive leadership team made up of the managing directors of five teams or businesses; Client Markets (CM), Finance, Products, Human Resources (HR) and Information Technology (IT). We'd sit around the table and agree on the expected budget for each business to attain a target premium for the business locally. That budget was then sent up to our Head Office in Brugge and they would collate it with the others and it would come back either approved or with a stretch goal in it. Once approved, each team would go back and set objectives for each of the individuals in the team and they'd be left alone for the year to run the budget, just reporting each quarter,'* she said.

Hanna valued the sense of autonomy this process gave. Her executive leadership team would decide together to move resources temporarily amongst the five businesses, thus helping each to meet the target objectives or stretch goals in the long term. As she explained,

'We'd say, OK we've got a couple of spare resources over there, we can move them over here and when that team's all right we can move them back. So we were much more business needs focussed in real time.'

This sense of supporting one another in building the business was important for Hanna.

'We came together when we weren't making money and we had to find a way to build people's competence in their teams without spending money. Rather than retrench people, all the managers worked co-operatively together with their teams, doing development exchanges across the teams. We weren't competing against each other. We had a communal goal', she reflected, going on to explain that *'everyone at every level knew where we were going. We educated people about how their team contributed to the result. In the first year we didn't make a profit, so the management team didn't take a bonus but gave it to the staff. If the goal was that 25% of business had to be new business, then teams would draft their own objectives about how they'd achieve that. The same target bonus system was in place for everyone, from the receptionist on, with all receiving the same percentage of their salary if the target was met.'*

Hanna spoke critically about the new structural arrangements.

'But what happens now is that someone else, somewhere else, makes decisions. There's a centralized executive team in Brugge that sends edicts directly out to each of the five departments and they each have to decide how to comply, whereas in the past this would go to the South Pacific division leadership team and we'd together manage the process. With this change we don't have target bonuses; we no longer have total control over the money. Now we (each department team) get mandates over night saying we have to cut expenses. So that forces your decision in a short period of time. You cut resources, cut expenses or sell more. There are only three options. And in a short period of time it's hard to sell more in the market we're in. So it puts a huge amount of pressure on you to make cuts. So you cut travel!'

The changes in structural arrangements have far reaching negative consequences, according to Hanna: *'What I see now is a different dynamic'*. She identified loss of autonomy, disruption of a sense of community

3. COMPLEXITY PHRASE SPACE

and lowered levels of trust, affecting the morale and culture of her division.

'My team reacts to this loss of autonomy. We have a "give me the parameters and I'll just get on and do it" mentality. The team works hard and plays hard. They find innovative ways to do things, all within the legal requirements. But they are more creative about how they do it and they don't respond well to rules and regulations.' She describes how the new system separates people rather than builds a sense of community. *'You have a low base wage and your pay goes up and down based on your results. It's very much a young people's scene – get in, do the deal, get out – and you get rewarded with really big bonuses. But our business is very much about relationships so it's a difficult environment to run this merchant bank model in and people are struggling with it and leaving.'*

In her view, such changes generated further negative consequences by undermining trust in the relationships. As she reflects, *'There used to be a high level of trust. You'd know if someone said they'd do something, that they would do it. You didn't need to talk about it in detail. We had a survey done and the consultant said it was the highest level of trust he'd seen in a management team. Now the South Pacific manager has so little trust of the group that he would only OK an in-house Christmas party so that he could monitor the way the evening went. Then we had some coaching, and one of the issues that came up was trust. His issue about trust had permeated through the whole organisation.'*

In summing up the differences between the old and new forms of getting things done, Hanna says: *'It's hard in the new structure. You get lots of rules and regulations. Before, we'd just go with what we thought was needed. We didn't necessarily know how it was going to work in minute detail but it worked. Looking back you saw why and how it worked. Now we are in a group and we have to plan in minute detail. Before, we had those underlying principles and values on how we were going to treat people and they were really basic – tell people what you expect and give them the tools to do it. We rewarded them and we were transparent about this. We had good communication.'*

Despite these concerns, Hanna feels she has recently witnessed a change for the better in organisational dynamics: *'Then I saw a tipping point. It was when the new people talked about how they'd come together to do this deal, and it was really successful. I thought there is a new way forward. I could feel it. I thought, we'll be all right now.'*

3.5 A complexity analysis of fractal fragment (4)

In this fractal fragment, Lifeguard Internatioanal Insurance Company, Hanna and her division all show *self-organisation, dynamism* and *emergence*. The merger and re-structure of the Company evidences all three principles. Part of the *dynamism* experienced is the way various employees interact with the changes. There are differing d*ynamics* between, for example, Hanna and her new manager, the Head Office executive team, and heads of the regional divisions. From Hanna's telling of the story we get a glimpse of one *emergence* – new, successful ways of doing business, and Hanna's own recognition of this.

In Hanna's description about how LIIC used to get things done, we see glimpses of a number of *phrase spaces*: that of the South Pacific division's executive team of managing directors, individual teams (CM, Finance, Products, HR and IT) and the Company's Head Office in Brugge. Hanna describes the overall past *phrase space* of the South Pacific division as having a sense of democracy and friendship, of strong *communicative connectedness*, whereby the managing directors and team members worked cooperatively with the LIIC Head Office. Hanna describes three interconnecting *phrase spaces* here – that of the 'group of managing directors', as they discussed and evolved budget goals for each team, the' five teams' (CM, Finance, Products, HR and IT) and the 'Brugge Head Office'. From Hanna's perspective, these *phrase spaces* were characterised by an attitude of supportiveness that extended from the whole of the South Pacific division to Head Office. This indicates that there is a *fractal* relationship between the various levels of the LIIC, with the characteristic of supportiveness apparent within individual people, individual teams and the South Pacific division.

As well as an attitude of supportiveness, Hanna talks of the sense of autonomy she and the other managing directors and business teams felt in being able to manage their own budgets. It is clear from Hanna's narrative that there are two major *attractors* influencing the South Pacific division of the LIIC: supportiveness and autonomy. That past structural arrangements allowed for both contributed significantly to the positive quality of the *phrase space* of the past. Conversely, Hanna and her colleagues felt the new structural arrangements were an imposition that radically reduced their capacity to work autonomously and to support one another. Viewed in this light, it is little wonder that there was loss of morale and that many decided to leave the Company.

The teams and team leaders (managing directors) had maintained *communicative connectedness,* and there was, across the South Pacific division of the LIIC, a sense of community or coherence, of joint ownership of the enterprise, and high levels of trust between personnel and teams had developed concurrently. Conversely, the new structural arrangements, of teams and departments being more linearly dependent upon and directly answerable to Head Office, worked to lessen *communicative connectedness* across the South Pacific division. The new arrangements set up conditions detrimental to caring for local relationships. Loss of trust between colleagues, teams and divisions was thus to be expected.

The South Pacific division's practice of having the same target bonus system for all employees depicts a *fractal* rather than hierarchical approach. Seeing organisations as *fractally* organised raises moral questions about equitability – for to see the whole present in the individual is to see everybody as

> Loss of the equitable target bonus system... means treating employees very differently, as 'hands' or 'feet' of the organisation, there to do 'its' bidding rather than as inherently constituting the organisation itself (which *fractality* would have us do).

contributing to the welfare and development of the *fractal,* no matter what level is focussed upon. Loss of the equitable target bonus system means more than local loss of control over finance. It also means treating employees very differently, as 'hands' or 'feet' of the organisation, there to do 'its' bidding rather than as inherently constituting the organisation itself (which *fractality* would have us do). So, what is a likely outcome of this change in attitude? One is that the employees treated in this way will continue to behave as *fractals* and will themselves take on similar attitudes and behaviours, distancing themselves from the aims and objectives of the company and no longer identifying themselves as the LIIC and, perhaps, seeking new employment opportunities where their efforts will attract greater financial rewards.

The South Pacific division teams came together at a time when the company was not making substantial profits. The *initial conditions* were that, due to lack of available funding support, the managers decided to work cooperatively to develop employee competencies. This was achieved through the managers cooperatively sponsoring development exchanges across the teams. This background set in place habits of cooperation, mutual support, high levels of trust and a sense that all were together working towards a shared goal. These *initial conditions* continued to influence processes and practices of getting things done and the Company was structured so that geographic regions maintained a similar degree of autonomy. All this changed with the recent merger and restructure of the Company. The new structural arrangements cut across habitual ways of getting things done. The strength of a sense of despondency felt by Hanna and others who left the LIIC can be in part explained by these *initial conditions*. If the *initial conditions* had been different (such as there being a feeling of competition or inequity at the local level) then the reaction to the new structural arrangements would have been different.

It is clear that Hanna had taken a *chaotic edge* stance to the changes. She saw the new way of operating, whereby power and control was invested differently via a centralised executive team in Brugge, as undermining the sense of participation in a shared enterprise and the autonomy of the South Pacific division and associated business teams. Hanna believed that these changes threatened the liveliness and success of her team and division, and would lead to eventual catastrophe for the LIIC. However, after seeing a successful outcome of how, in a different way, the new people were able to come together to *'do this deal'* and so create new business, Hanna came to an *edge of chaos* appreciation of the changes in organisational processes and practices, recognising them as indications of the self-organising dynamism and emergence of the LIIC.

So, from the perspective of this complexity analysis, how could the merger and restructure have been handled differently to minimise the anxiety or *chaotic edge* thinking of the South Pacific division? Some suggestions are:

1. Involve the participants of the South Pacific division in the process of evolving or planning the new structural and reporting arrangements. In other words, let these people co-participate in creating the new *phrase space*. Here the 'them' becomes 'us'.
2. Put in place a number of strategies for maintaining *communicative connectedness* between the Brugge executive team and the managing directors for each of the geographical divisions. This could take the form of regular (weekly or monthly) conversational exchanges (email, skype, teleconferences or face to face meetings) to provide an opportunity to maintain the sense of a trustworthy relationship between the members across the various divisions of the LIIC. In this way, small autopoietic loops may be generated that foster coherence between the self-producing and self-organising processes of individuals, the teams and the sections and to the whole of the LIIC.

3. Include in the *phrase space* discussion consideration of the importance of *sensitive dependence on initial conditions.* For example, bring into the conversation a recognition and appreciation of South Pacific cultural norms and *attractors* (such as valuing the ability to work autonomously and to support others) together with the significant *initial conditions* relating to other areas of the LIIC (such as the cultural norms of organisations and people in Belgium).
4. The Brugge executive team should pay attention to *fractal* indicators across the organisation, recognising that many of the aspirations, attitudes and concerns expressed at one site of the LIIC are likely to be replicated elsewhere. An unhappy receptionist may indicate frustration felt by others. Bearing in mind *sensitive dependence on initial conditions*, to ignore this may be perilous for the company. Remember *a kingdom was lost. All for want of a nail.*

3.6 *From complexity-based analysis to complexity-inspired ways of organising*

The complexity-based analysis presented above demonstrates how issues and problems commonly encountered can be effectively reinterpreted from a complexity perspective. By providing examples of how the metaphors can be used to analyse organisational processes and practices, I trust I have made it easier for you to engage with complexity habits of thought and to gain some confidence in your own capacity to use complexity to create new understandings and approaches to your own experiences in organisations. A complexity approach constitutes a way of not limiting imagination in working with organisational forms, processes and practices. Often structure is seen as a panacea, the assumption being that getting the

> A complexity approach constitutes a way of not limiting imagination in working with organisational forms, processes and practices.

structure 'right' will solve difficulties. However, as we repeatedly find out, new structures generate new sets of restrictions and thereby new difficulties. Complexity, in contrast, emphasises that attitudes, habits of thought and communicative processes are critical to success, and that careful attention to these will generate processes supportive of a flourishing emergence.

Further reading

Complexity and science

Bak, P. and Chen, K. (1991) 'Self-organised Criticality', *Scientific American*. January 1991.

Jones, R. (1983) *Physics as Metaphor.* London: ABACUS.

Langton, C. (1986) 'Studying Artificial Life with Cellular Automata', *Physica* 22D: 120-49.

Mandelbrot, B. (1977) *The Fractal Geometry of Nature.* New York: Freeman.

Maturana, H. and Varela, F. (1987) *The Tree of Knowledge.* Boston, MA: Shambhala.

Packard, N. (1988) 'Adaptation Towards the Edge of Chaos', Technical Report, Center for Complex Systems research, University of Illinois, CCSR-88-5.

Wilkinson, M. (Environmental Editor) (2008) 'Cold Rush for Arctic's Energy Riches', *The Sydney Morning Herald* 4 August 2008

Wolfram,S.(2002) *A New Kind of Science.* Champaign, IL: Wolfram Media

Vickers, G. (1984) *Human Systems are Different.* London: Harper and Row.

Complexity and organisations

Kuhn, L. and Woog, R. (2007) 'From complexity concepts to creative applications', *World Futures: The Journal of General Evolution.* Vol 63, Nos 3-4, April-June.pp.176-193.

Kuhn, L., Woog, R. and Hodgson, M. (2003) 'Applying complexity principles to enhance organisational knowledge management', *Proceedings, Global Business and Technology Association Conference: Challenging the Frontiers in Global Business and Technology: Implementation of Changes in Values, Strategies and Policy.* Budapest, Hungary, July 8-11, pp. 754-762.

Shaw, P. (2002) *Changing Conversations in Organisations.* London: Routledge.

Stacey, R. D., Griffin, D. and Shaw, P. (2000) *Complexity and Management.* London: Routledge.

About organisations

Boje, D. M. (2001) *Narrative Methods for Organisational and Communications Research.* London: Sage.

Denning, S. (2000) *The Springboard: How Storytelling Ignites Action in Knowledge.* London: Butterworth-Heinemann.

Gould, R. (2007) 'Voices from the past, heard in the present, beckoning the future', Honours Thesis, University of Western Sydney, Australia.

Nonaka, I. (2004) 'A dynamic theory of organisational knowledge creation', Starkey, K., Tempest, S. and McKinlay, A. (ed's) *How Organisations Learn.* London: Thomson.

Weick, K. (1995) *Sensemaking in Organisations.* London: Sage.

Wenger, E. (2004) 'Communities of Practice and Social Learning Systems', Starkey, K., Tempest, S. and McKinlay, A. (ed's) *How Organisations Learn.* London: Thomson.

Woog, R. (2004) 'The Knowing of Knowledge', *Australian National Training Authority (2004) Working and Learning in Vocational Education and Training in the Knowledge Era.* Available at http://www.flexiblelearning.net.au/projects/resources/PDFutureF.doc

Philosophically interesting

Rorty, R. (1998) *Truth and Progress, Philosophical Papers Vol 3.* Cambridge: Cambridge University Press.

Tutu, D. (1999) *No Future Without Forgiveness.* London: Rider.

Wittgenstein, L. (1988) *Tractatus Logico-Philosophicus.* Trans. Pears, D. F. and McGuiness, B.F. London: Routledge and Humanities Press International.

Poetry, arts and literature

Blake, W. (1994) *Selected Poems.* (Ed I. Hamilton). London: Bloomsbury Publishing.

Lopate, P. (1995) *The Art of the personal Essay: An Anthology from the Classic Era to the Present.* New York: Anchor Book, Doubleday

Rilke, R. M. (2004) *Letters to a Young Poet.* (Trans. M. D. Herter Norton) London: W. W. Norton and Company

Robinson, J. A. (1981) 'Personal Narratives Reconsidered', *Journal of American Folklore, 94:58-85.*

Winterson, J. (2005) *Weight.* Melbourne: The text Publishing Company.

Psychologically interesting

Jung, C. G. (1995) *Memories, Dreams, Reflections.* London: Fontana Press.

Kelly, G. (1955) *The Psychology of Personal Constructs Vol 1 and 2.* New York: W. W. Norton and Company.

Vygotsky, L. (1978) *Mind in Society: The Development of Higher Psychological Processes.* Cambridge: Harvard University Press.

4. IDENTIFYING PATTERNS AND POTENTIALITY

4.1 Complexity-based pattern analysis

The basic organising principles of a complexity cosmography, together with seven complexity metaphors, have been introduced and discussed in the preceding chapters in order to show how a complexity-based view of organisational life approaches understanding of organisational forms, processes and practices from a new direction.

To reiterate, self-organisation, dynamism and emergence were presented as basic organising principles that are applicable universally to all organic entities, regardless of scale. Within organisations, self-organisation, dynamism and emergence were shown as characteristics essential to individual people, groups, divisions and so on.

The seven complexity metaphors have been introduced, discussed and demonstrated through a selection of fractal fragments. I chose *fitness landscape, phase space – phrase space, communicative connectedness, sensitive dependence on initial conditions, edge of chaos – chaotic edge, attractors and fractality,* from a far longer list of possibilities, simply because I have found them useful in revealing the topography of networks and processes that constitute organisational life.

> ... [*fractal fragments* as] narrative accounts... represent only a minute proportion of the narratives relating to each organisation... telling much but not all... [they] are *fractal*, as they indicate simultaneously similar experiences across multiple sites.

Having explained the nature of *fractality*, the reasons for my use of the term *fractal fragment* for the vignettes or narrative accounts presented throughout the book may now be clear. I see these as *fragments* of narratives as they represent only a minute proportion of the narratives relating to each organisation. They are similar to a snapshot in time, telling much but not all. These fragments are *fractal*, as they indicate simultaneously similar experiences across multiple sites. So, when I wrote in the first chapter of Anna's experience of self-organisation within a deeply

4. IDENTIFYING PATTERNS AND POTENTIALITY

hierarchical organisation, I see her experience as replicated across a range of departments, organisations, sectors and so on. In telling stories gathered from a range of practitioners grappling with the tensions and complications inherent in their organisations, I assume that they are not alone in toiling in these ways and that their reflections may be useful for others working in comparably messy and complex situations.

Illustrative complexity-based analytical descriptions of fractal fragments from Outreach Loans Bank, the Liverpool Catholic Club and Lifeguard International Insurance Company have been included in the two previous chapters. The analytical description of Jay and Bilal's experiences with Outreach Loans Bank illustrates a way of working with the principles of self-organisation, dynamism and emergence and the metaphor of fitness landscape. The analytical descriptions developed for Ryan's research into the Liverpool Catholic Club and Hanna's narrative about Lifeguard International Insurance Company illustrate the complexity principles and all seven metaphors.

In this chapter, a range of ways of working with complexity will be introduced and demonstrated. I will begin by introducing three complexity-based inquiry methods – *coherent conversations*, *fractal analysis* and *attractor analysis*. I then develop illustrative analytical descriptions for another three fractal fragments, with the emphasis this time on demonstrating how applied complexity-based pattern analysis identifies underlying patterns of order together with indications of possible future emergences. Understanding such underlying patterns provides an effective way of identifying what is involved in determining how an organisation self-organises. From such analysis we gain insight into why particular ways of organising to get things done arise and persist in organisations and why translating practices and techniques that work in one setting to another is so often a risky and unsatisfying experience.

> From such [complexity-based pattern] analysis we gain insight into why particular ways of organising to get things done arise and persist in organisations....

The fractal fragments presented in this chapter differ from those of the previous chapters because here each fractal fragment constitutes in itself an illustrative analysis and demonstrates how complexity habits of thought have been utilised in identifying pattern and potentiality. Each of the three fractal fragments included relate not only to different types of organisation but also to different approaches to identification of pattern and potentiality.

> By offering a series of illustrative descriptive analyses, I want to indicate something of what is involved in undertaking a complexity-based analysis.

By offering a series of illustrative descriptive analyses, I want to indicate something of what is involved in undertaking a complexity-based analysis. However, it is important to recognise that there is a limit to what can be spelled out in terms of 'how to do it'. There is much that cannot be completely explained, simply because of the nature of human activity and sense-making. In the end, there remains that which cannot be codified, that which resists explicit explanation. By presenting a series of analyses, I hope to provide directions through which you can imaginatively engage complexity approaches appropriate to your own interests and concerns.

> ... I hope to provide directions through which you can imaginatively engage complexity approaches appropriate to your own interests and concerns.

In concluding the chapter, I describe two further ways that my colleagues and I work with complexity. The final two sections draw together complexity habits of thought and philosophical, psychological and sociological insights. These sections are included for two reasons: 1) to provide useful models for identification of pattern and potentiality and 2) to demonstrate ways in which you may bring theories, ideas or insights with which you are familiar to your engagement with complexity.

4.2   *Complexity-based inquiry methods*

So far I have said very little about the inquiry methods that were used to generate the fractal fragments other than to say that they are based on interviews with people who were invited to relate poignant stories about the practices through which their organisation typically 'gets things done'. Let me provide some explanation of how the interviews were conducted.

4.2.1 Coherent conversations

I employed a complexity-based approach to the interviews, conducting each as a coherent conversation, a research method developed by my colleagues and me (Kuhn, Woog and Knox 2006, Kuhn and Woog 2007). Coherent conversations may take place as one-to-one interviews or group conversations. As group conversations they can be thought of as similar in structure to focus groups. However, whereas a focus group aims to have a conversation about a particular topic, coherent conversations aim to hold a permissive conversation, one that accepts the entirety of topics that people bring into the conversation and which is critically self-reflective of the processes via which the conversation emerges. As an inquiry method, coherent conversations have the following characteristics. They:

- are permissive not agenda bound, allowing people's priorities and own agendas to emerge;
- may reveal the way people think, as much as what they say;
- make the conversational dynamics and relationships as apparent as everything that is being said;
- are self-reflective of the conversational process;
- are both intuitive and logical.

> Whereas designed situation interventions are outcome driven, coherent conversations create enhanced potentiality... [and] facilitate emergence by generating conditions that are supportive of further developments.

In organisational settings, coherent conversations can be used as an inquiry method that facilitates emergence. Whereas designed situation interventions are outcome-driven, coherent conversations create enhanced potentiality. A complexity perspective sees organisations as processes of communication and joint action (Griffin 2002) – networks of relationships shaped by *communicative connectedness*. Coherent conversations facilitate emergence by generating conditions that are supportive of further developments. They do this in two important ways. First, they build coherent understanding and thus strengthen *communicative connectedness* and, secondly, they reveal and help establish *phrase space*.

4. IDENTIFYING PATTERNS AND POTENTIALITY

Much can be learned from the narratives generated through coherent conversations by applying two complexity-based analytical techniques: *fractal analysis* and *attractor analysis*.

4.2.2 Fractal analysis

Viewing organisations as fractally constructed means looking for similarities that are apparent across different scales. From the study of one fractal (for example, an individual or department) we can make generalisations about much larger phenomena (such as the organisation as a whole, or the sectors across which it operates) from which the fractal is derived.

By examining the narratives for views or concerns that are repeatedly expressed, we can glimpse the macrocosm, despite the proportional limitation of the scale we are dealing with (as represented by the individuals or groups involved). For an organisation this means that one can expect to see revealed in the narrative of one group, such as a certain task-related team, views held by other teams at both micro and macro scales. So, by paying attention to the concerns of mobile lenders for the south-western region of Outreach Loans Bank, we can be sure that some of their concerns will be replicated elsewhere, such as at the level of board membership for the south-western region or the Australian financial market in general. It is important to understand that the fractal selected for study (such as mobile lenders for the south-western region of Outreach Loans Bank) is not merely a part of the whole but, in important ways, is representative of the whole.

Through taking a fractal approach, we can study and make sense of small portions of the organisation without artificially simplifying these. Smaller scale fractals remain equally complex microcosms of the whole. The capacity for self-organisation and emergence in one fractal represents the dynamics and capacity for emergence of the system as a whole.

4. IDENTIFYING PATTERNS AND POTENTIALITY

4.2.3 Attractor analysis

Like fractal analysis, *attractor analysis* enables us to make sense of narratives without overly simplifying these. In looking for *attractors* we aim to identify the values, issues of concern, motivators and so on that guide and shape attitudes and behaviours. It is important that the narratives have been generated through permissive rather than tightly prescribed conversations because, to identify *attractors*, we need to glimpse something of why people hold their views and attitudes. It is in the 'why' that the *attractors* are revealed. Identifying the *attractor* or *attractor* set assists us in building a broad understanding of the complex system, extending beyond the group of people involved in the coherent conversation. Understanding what guides the attitudes and behaviours of those involved, we can make inferences about the self-organising character of the system.

> It is important that the narratives have been generated through permissive rather than tightly prescribed conversations because, to identify *attractors*, we need to glimpse something of why people hold their views and attitudes. It is in the 'why' that the *attractors* are revealed.

Paying attention to *attractors,* we can gain insight about possible changes. There is some sense of predictability associated with social entities (individuals, teams, departments, whole organisations, sectors and so on) undergoing critical transitions in *phase space* – moving from one *attractor* to another. Although it is hard to know when the transition will occur, symptoms of instability, such as rapidly increasing complexity and the appearance of chaotic dynamics, serve as indicators of approaching transition. The emerging neophyte shape of a new *attractor* may also be used to speculate about likely ongoing development and its ultimate character.

4.2.4 Useful questions for complexity-informed inquirers

For those wanting further hints about how to undertake a complexity-based inquiry into a specific organisational setting, I suggest that a useful starting point would be to compile a series of questions about the organisational forms, processes and practices, such as those indicated in the list below. Remember, these

4. IDENTIFYING PATTERNS AND POTENTIALITY

questions are suggestions and are included here merely as a stimulus to your own thinking.

What indications and characteristics of self-organisation are apparent?

What dynamics are evident? Who relates to whom?

How may interactions be characterised?

What indications of emergence are apparent?

How may its phase space be depicted?

What are the characteristics of its phrase spaces?

What indicators are there of the qualities of communicative connectedness?

What instances of influential initial conditions can you discern?

What has happened in the recent history of the organisation?

How would you describe the organisation's fitness landscape? What recent peaks and troughs are apparent?

How is edge of chaos or the chaotic edge played out?

Who takes which perspective and in relation to what?

What are the major attractors around which the organisation's evolution unfolds?

What fractal characteristics are apparent?

4.3   *Enhancing knowledge management at Multi-national Pharmaceuticals: fractal fragment (5)*

This fractal fragment is presented in a different manner from those I have thus far introduced. It sets out, in effect, two fractal narratives. One relates to the research process, illustrating how complexity-based inquiry processes may be utilised. The second narrative concerns knowledge management requirements and practices and the implications of these for encouraging and developing creativity.

A few years ago some colleagues and I undertook research into how creativity might be encouraged and developed in organisations (Kuhn, Woog and Hodgson 2003). The CEO and senior management team of Multi-national Pharmaceuticals invited us to work with them because they wanted to learn more about how Multi-national Pharmaceuticals could maintain a peak position within its fitness landscape. We used the complexity-based inquiry methods as described above (coherent conversations, fractal and *attractor* analysis) to explore the way that creativity was galvanised within the company.

The project was based on the assumptions that:

- if managers better understood what was involved, they could improve their own creativity and foster increased creativity across the organisation;
- creativity within an organisation is related to knowledge management practices;
- insight into the motivations guiding knowledge management practices would provide insight into how to better foster creativity;
- knowledge can be described as 'borrowed' when it is categorised and stored, and as 'generated' when it is created by the individuals involved and does not exist outside of the organisation.

We hypothesised that it would be useful to explore how borrowed knowledge interacts over time with generated knowledge and how this generated knowledge is recognised and valued.

We held individual coherent conversations with 14 senior managers, asking them to reflect on their ideas about knowing, knowledge, creativity and innovation. We then involved the managers in two days of research interventions where we exposed them to learning experiences that deliberately stimulated the interface between borrowed and generated knowledge. The interventions included introducing new theoretical concepts through lectures and non-directed discussions and participation in team-based activities. The interface between borrowed and generated knowledge was stimulated by introducing new theories, concepts and activities, requiring the managers to make sense of these by integrating the new with their already held understandings of organisation-related issues. Following this, in a second two-day cooperative research phase, the senior managers and ourselves engaged in a large group-reflective coherent conversation, jointly making sense of and, in effect, creating the findings of the project. Here the distinction between researcher and 'research participant' was blurred. All of the activities and conversations were recorded and analysed for indications of *fractality* and for the identification of *attractors*.

Throughout the project we engaged in conversation with the managers, evoking their narratives about creativity, innovation, knowledge and knowing. Coherent conversations as utilised in this project accomplished two tasks. First, they provided a means for us to gain access to the *life-world* and views of the participants (senior managers of Multi-national Pharmaceuticals). Secondly, participation facilitated emergence by enhancing *communicative connectedness* between the managers and revealing to them the nature of their *phrase space* in relation to creativity and knowledge management.

The following three sample narratives responding to the question 'What does creativity mean to you?' indicate the range of ways by which creativity was understood by the senior managers.

Summing up her view, Anneke reflected: *'We are always being asked to be "creative". Like 3M and Micro-soft. Yeah, as if! My science background didn't allow or encourage creativity and besides, if I was the creative type, then I wouldn't have done science would I? I'd be an artist, a musician or a poet. And what's more, my organisation doesn't seriously encourage creativity, with its focus on complying with protocols and that's really important in a pharmaceutical company. If people don't follow the processes then the senior managers get very niggly. Work is too busy for creativity. There's too much to do. The routine of everyday office life rules – people would think you are wasting time if you just sat staring into space.'*

Bede took a different perspective, saying *'I wouldn't consider myself as a particularly creative person, except in terms of my ability to look for creative solutions to problems – I'm good at problem solving. I'm most creative when I'm interacting with others. I get different opinions and thoughts leading me to think about other things that I may not have thought about. But at the same time I feel people who are very rigid in their thinking hamper my creativity. I like working with Wayne, our Associate Manager – he's a very methodological type of guy, but he's also prepared to think outside the square a little bit. I like people to consider all options before they disregard them. People who aren't prepared to even toss an idea on the board, who write something off before they have given the idea a chance to float, frustrate me and inhibit my creativity and the more anxious I get, the less likely I am to come up with a suitable solution.'*

Colette's reflections add another dimension. As she explained: *'I see creativity as looking at things from a different perspective and challenging the status quo. In an organisation, it should give you a competitive advantage either by creating a distinct product or by improving the way you do things. It's not enough to 'be creative'; it has to lead to innovation. I think creativity is a necessity for me, being an engineer. To be creative you need a bit of a catalyst – a need has to be identified first. You also have to have access to finances that you can give people to play with. It's up to me how much I am affected by knowing that we have to stay within a budget and that the success of my creativity affects my bonus. Sometimes that's irrelevant to what you want to get out of it at the end. But sometimes budget and bonus stay in the back of my mind influencing the creative process.'*

These three responses are broadly indicative of those of the whole group of 14 senior managers. These responses can be described as fractal because others

4. IDENTIFYING PATTERNS AND POTENTIALITY

> These responses can be described as fractal because others (such as those working in different domains – innovation and development, business operations, engineering solutions and so on) repeated the understandings across the organisation.

(such as those working in different domains – innovation and development, business operations, engineering solutions and so on) repeated the understandings across the organisation. Looking at the totality of responses, and following the large group reflective coherent conversation of the second workshop, 15 fractal themes were identified that related to the way that creativity was galvanised within Multi-national Pharmaceuticals. These were:

1. Understanding of creativity is multifaceted. Creativity represents the exotic other, the artistic, as well as an everyday purpose-driven occurrence.
2. Conversation and language is critical to recognising and generating creativity.
3. Creativity means doing something different that is aimed at achieving a goal or an improvement.
4. Individuals are creative, and they are creative in relationship.
5. Forms of creativity vary with the environmental context.
6. Within the work situation creativity is bounded and therefore potentially limited.
7. Certain conditions are necessary for a person or group to be creative: a triggering need or challenge, permission and/or encouragement (of colleagues and bosses), exposure to otherness, physical and mental space, and a measure of freedom.
8. Creativity is limited by: organisational values, processes that schedule creativity, processes that keep things the same, lack of personal and/or group autonomy, lack of trust, lack of confidence, busyness and stress, and rigid adherence to procedure.
9. Creativity is influenced by fear of failure.
10. Creativity is influenced by the sensitivity of the human soul or psyche mitigating against public debate of issues.

93

11. For creativity to occur there needs to be space for the unknown, a chasm to be bridged.
12. Too much uncertainty, or having too many complicating variables, hinders creativity.
13. Perhaps the most powerful influence on creativity is the organisation's culture and politics.
14. Theoretical knowledge is not often utilised as a source of new ideas.
15. Theories, ideas and concepts are only of interest if their source is trustworthy, and if the material is immediately useful. The perceived validity of a theory equates with its perceived usefulness.

We (researchers and managers together) then composed an indicative narrative representing the whole. Written as one person's story yet containing all the fractal themes, this can be described as a fractal narrative about creativity and innovation, and all of the issues relating to how creativity is encouraged or discouraged within Multi-national Pharmaceuticals are apparent. In reflecting the totality of views, this fractal narrative served to enhance the participants' understanding of their own situation. It provided individuals with a larger picture and became a basis upon which to further build *communicative connectedness* across the organisation.

The full indicative narrative follows.

INDICATIVE NARRATIVE of Multi-national Pharmaceuticals

You asked me about creativity. It's not something that I think about. Together with goodness, usefulness, cleverness, you take it for granted that you know and do those things instinctively. Creativity! I wonder why they want to know? Is this the brainchild of one of the HR gurus? Who knows?

For better or for worse, I said that I'd be in this, so let me think about it. Creativity is something that I think of in relation to the arts, music and literature. Creative people are usually a bit exotic; they have a dreadful sense of fashion and are not all that keen on a hair cut. That's a bit judgemental. But, seriously, creativity can have an everyday face. My creativity doesn't look exotic it's just something that's new, a new way of doing things, new ideas. It's what happens when people flourish.

For me to be creative I need to feel that no-one is watching over my shoulder, and that I don't get criticism and knocks if someone doesn't like what I'm doing or if my creative direction turns out not to be as rewarding as we had all hoped. I guess freedom is important; it's very hard to be creative if you are fearful that, if there is a glitch along the process, someone is going to kick you in the arse. You play it safe. You test it a dozen times over. You don't say 'hey! I want to have a go at this' or 'how about we do it this way'. Instead you are circumspect. You hedge your commitment and your exposure in lots of ways. You say perhaps, maybe, somehow, what would you think, wouldn't it be interesting and you always, in this way, maintain at least an arm's length, if not a boot's length, from the creative idea. I wonder whether there'd be any creativity if you weren't so confident or courageous enough to give it a go.

There is a small handful of people that I trust and enjoy working with. And when we come together we are creative. Creativity seems to be built around differences in group discussion or just in conversation. It's a process of being open and questioning and being supportive when you've reached a new insight or understanding. It is difficult to discern, in this process, who has added which idea. It's a collective development and ownership of the creative outcome. So you don't have to be concerned about saying something outlandish or that you will be reprimanded or ridiculed for having a go. Sometimes this is done informally without the declaration that we are going through a creative process. It happens when you are chatting in a car, having a drink — probably more often when having a drink than in any other situation.

Now on the other hand, if you declare that you will bring out creativity and there will be a workshop under the dopey guidance of someone else, you may as well kiss creativity goodbye. It's hard to be creative when you are dancing the steps of someone else's creative agenda.

It's not hard to see how we can pay lip service to creativity but not create the climate in which it can flourish. If you are scared of offending someone, wandering into someone else's territory, while seeking to please everyone who wants a say in the matter at the same time, let me tell you — that's when you can't be creative. You can't be creative if you're dog-tired either. Now here is an interesting piece of speculation. Do we get overloaded at work to make sure we are dog-tired? Then the organisation can say, they had every opportunity to be creatively involved, they just haven't made a contribution. So there is the evidence. You can provide all the opportunities you like, but in the end,

Cont. overleaf

4. IDENTIFYING PATTERNS AND POTENTIALITY

we - us, the senior managers, the executives - have to carry the burden of creativity. I wonder if they know what they are doing or whether they are so clueless that they just do it anyway. No, they are not doing it consciously, they are not creative enough to do so! They just measure life and progress in terms of production and the need to have guidelines and procedures to keep our production momentum on course.

My creativity is a longing. It's a drive to face challenges, to cope with some of the unknowns, and in doing so, to achieve and improve in ways that support me as a person so that I feel that I am successful in my work with the organisation. It's an opportunity to show my full potential as a human being. Creativity then is not all that different inside or outside my work. It's a desire, a drive, a way of being. However, at work, creativity is more easily named and recognised, whereas outside work, it just takes place and may not have even been noticed.

We've started to use the term 'moving from equilibrium to the edge of chaos'. I'll come up with my own terms, and add to the repertoire of terms and phrases that seem so popular around here. Creativity is a guided wildness. Why is it wildness? Because it requires a degree of risk and adventure, of letting go, and almost a sense of bravado in that, come what may, I will follow the excitement. There is a vitality associated with creativity; a sense of being alive and on the edge. It's wild, because it will irritate and offend, even if you're very careful. Funny that: people seem to be irritated whenever you move off the familiar and the known. This might be jealousy or maybe an in-built safety mechanism for all of us. Never mind - there has to be a degree of risk-taking, irritation and hope. There is also a sense of wildness in approaching the 'edge of chaos', looking the uncontrollable and the unpredictable in the face.

Guided? It's guided because we always operate in pre-determined and existent environments and settings. Inside Multi-national Pharmaceuticals, you can't, in all honesty, cut across powerful people or dogmatic and traditional procedural lines - and you'd be a fool to do so. Creativity seems to be limited by having to appear to be busy at work, by having to fit it into a schedule. But life outside isn't all that different. Try crossing powerful and dogmatic rules, which they call, in some cases, breaking the law. There are other rules that relate to friends and family. Think seriously about offending powerful others, like one's partner or children or even the bank manager!

Power and politics would appear to me to be the most influential elements in affecting creativity in Multi-national Pharmaceuticals. Politics may range from subtle inter relational dynamics to the guiding rules of the organisation. At the large scale, it's more visible. We, the organisation, stand for this ... we believe in this ...organise ourselves for these purposes. But the personal level is more influential. Have I offended someone? Can I keep my colleagues' respect and trust? How far can I go in exerting my individuality, in emphasising my differentness but maintaining my belongingness and membership of my peer group that determines the quality of my day-to-day work life? I have to pay homage to the gurus in New York, but I need to have someone to have lunch with in the cafeteria in Ryde. Inasmuch as I can do that, I am a real creative person.

So that's what creativity means to me!

4. IDENTIFYING PATTERNS AND POTENTIALITY

So, did we learn how knowledge management could be enhanced so as to better foster creativity? We did. Our conclusion was that Multi-national Pharmaceuticals' *phrase space* (within the context of creativity and knowledge management) was shaped by the way the managers reflected their individually understood ideas and theories about creativity and innovation. The 15 identified fractal themes, and the indicative narrative, depict the *phrase space* of the organisation (within the context of creativity and knowledge). This *phrase space* contains and constrains the specific character of the organisation's dynamics, the behavioural orientations of all involved, the favoured interpretations of ideas, and the attitudes to knowledge and knowledge management within which individuals and sections operate.

Paying attention to the *phrase space* of Multi-national Pharmaceuticals provided us with a basis for a better understanding of the ways by which generated and borrowed knowledge sourcing, development and use is understood and approached within this organisation. The fractal themes indicate that there is a tension within Multi-national Pharmaceuticals' *phrase space* in relation to creativity and knowledge management. On the one hand, knowledge is valued according to how immediately applicable and useful it is thought to be. On the other hand, for creativity to flourish there must be tolerance for uncertainty and the unknown and support for free exploration, even when this does not appear to lead to immediately applicable outcomes. The *phrase space*, in this sense, is seen to be organised around a pairing of *attractors*, one guiding towards behaviours that would generate immediately applicable knowledge and the other guiding towards tolerance for free exploration. Although the fractal themes relate specifically to perceptions about creativity and innovation, we were able to deduce ideas from them to improve *phrase space* support for generated knowledge initiatives, so that creativity and innovation could be enhanced.

> ... for creativity to flourish there must be tolerance for uncertainty and the unknown and support for free exploration, even when this does not appear to lead to immediately applicable outcomes.

We concluded that Multi-national Pharmaceuticals was operating at the *edge of chaos* if both borrowed and generated knowledge were seen as important for competitive advantage, learning and growth. At the *edge of chaos*, risk is construed as necessary experimentation, there is tolerance for lack of compliance, and goals are not always linked to predicted output measures. Operating with an *edge of chaos* attitude is supportive of knowledge expansion in organisations but not necessarily supportive of codification and the technological management of explicit knowledge.

Conversely, operating at the *chaotic edge* describes an alternate, reactive approach to managing knowledge. Here there is little tolerance for new ideas and internally generated knowledge, and compliance to process and behavioural norms is stressed. Goals have a strong output definition, and a mantra to stick to core activities and functional focus is heard. Knowledge is valued and accepted for its current utility and immediate applicability. At the *chaotic edge*, borrowed knowledge is favoured for being tried and tested, for being familiar and reliable. It has privilege over generated knowledge. To minimise risk and maximise control and compliance, the focus is on capturing and institutionalising borrowed knowledge. Taking a *chaotic edge* stance, borrowed knowledge will be 'tightly held' by the organisation as being 'the right way'. So, a *chaotic edge* attitude to knowledge management actively mitigates encouraging creativity.

We identified six factors contributing to the *phrase space* of Multi-national Pharmaceuticals, which would determine whether it was characterised as *edge of chaos* or *chaotic edge*. These were:

1. *Risk Tolerance*: How much is risk tolerated or embraced?
2. *Output Orientation*: What level of goal and output orientation is there and what requirement is there for specific measurable outputs for activities?
3. *Institutional Compliance*: What level of demand for compliance to institutionalised process, language and behaviour is there?

4. *Individual Competitiveness*: How much does judgement and competition between individuals and organisational functions influence the underlying performance paradigm?
5. *Diversity Management*: Does the organisation manage diversity through cross-functional teams or through functionally constrained groups?
6. *Applicability Impetus*: How important is the utility and immediacy of knowledge?

The attitude taken to each of these factors can be described as giving shape to, or revealing the relative impact of, the two *attractors* around which the organisational processes and practices are organised. For example, we see the pull of the *attractor* for immediate applicable knowledge (and borrowed knowledge) when there is little tolerance for risk with a strong emphasis on achieving specific goals and complying with organisational protocols, and the pull of the *attractor* for free exploration (and hence support of generated knowledge) when there is tolerance for taking risks, a relaxed attitude towards compliance to institutionalised protocols and flexibility around meeting specific goals.

By paying attention to how they were constructing their *phrase space* in terms of these six factors, the managers became better informed about how their knowledge management practices function in relation to their own attitudes and ways of talking. We found, too, that the quality of *communicative connectedness* among those involved determined whether an *edge of chaos* or *chaotic edge* perspective came to be the '*modus operandi*'. Rewarding, trusting relationships and energetic self-organising communication that enhances *communicative connectedness* was seen as supportive of greater risk tolerance, flexibility around meeting goals, a more relaxed attitude to compliance and so on. As previously noted, communication and relationships really matter in complex systems. In understanding these points, the managers became more knowledgeable about how to actively encourage creativity in their organisation. Thus the potential of Multi-national Pharmaceuticals for maintaining and developing fitness peaks was enhanced.

4.4. Fractal fragment (6) Phil, The KIA Group

This fractal fragment is based on conversations with Phil who, at the time of the interview, was the operations manager for KIA-Contractors, one of a group of companies called The KIA Group. KIA, Kiwis in Australia, was the acronym used by the Group chairman, John Williams, when the company formed because it depicted the labour force that is utilised in its operations. As Phil was completing a higher degree in social inquiry at the time and has a special interest in social applications and developments of complexity, his narrative depicts and illustrates a complexity-based style of making sense. His narrative shows the kinds of insights into pattern and potentiality possible when a person is familiar with complexity.

Phil explained that The KIA Group began about 10 years ago with a group of guys forming a labour supply company for unpacking containers at the wharves. The KIA Group has now grown into a multimillion-dollar enterprise through expansion into other service areas such as Logistics, Warehousing, Recruitment and Telecommunications.

KIA-Contractors supply labour crews for container packing and unpacking. They make contractual arrangements with importers and warehousing companies that have storage at wharves or in business park locations situated around key ports and railway yards. Phil's role is to look after the operations of the labour force. In an area that is highly unpredictable and hugely unstable, he is responsible for placing labour in areas where it is needed, maintaining a labour force that enables the company to deal with the ups and downs of work demands and, at the same time, trying to achieve an income for the company. In Phil's view this means his work is positioned *'right at the edge of chaos'*.

Ships arrive in Australia bringing goods from overseas. Phil organises crews (fork lift operators and general labourers) to meet ships at the wharves, or trains at railway yards, to unpack the containers. As the amount of goods arriving fluctuates with the ups and downs of the Australian economy and its consumption patterns, as well as with factors beyond (such as overseas labour concerns, complexities with the manufacturing process and so on), the demand for labour is similarly fluctuating and unstable. KIA-Contractors has an agreement with each client that they will get the products into the client's warehouse within a certain period of time and at an agreed-upon price, regardless of potential complications such as petrol price changes. Phil's role is to maintain the best possible fitness landscape for KIA-Contractors, balancing labour requirements, satisfactory completion of client contracts, maintenance of suitable potential employees and profit margins for the company.

Phil told me that he finds that the complexity principles and metaphors perfectly describe his experiences and the context within which KIA-Contractors operates. Working with complexity habits of thought helps him in his understanding of his role as operations manager and in his capacity to work more effectively.

To illustrate what he's dealing with, Phil told me about his past week: *'Just this week we have experienced chaos. New clients emerged from a stack of quotes given out and they wanted their orders fulfilled almost immediately. Just prior to this news, two key crewmembers left – one because of personal problems and the other to go to greener pastures. This left us short of skilled labour in the key area of crew management. What had been a very quiet business period suddenly changed to where we were receiving orders from established customers as well as the demands of the new clients. And then the company chairman called and said that, because of the downturn in our overall profits, we will all have to take salary cuts till it picks up.'*

Reflecting on the situation, Phil remarked: *'What some may refer to as 'Murphy's Law' is just complexity at its best or worst, depending on one's perspective. What is helpful is to know that one cannot control all situations within the workplace; that's life, it's sometimes chaotic. Spending lots of energy trying to control is fraught with disappointments. To cope with the challenges that I face, I find that I need to constantly focus on broadening my communication, relational and motivational skills. It is only through this that the organisation can jump to new levels of performance.'*

I was keen to find out more about how Phil's familiarity with complexity principles and metaphors is translated into practice. Phil's explanation of the work processes that he sets up makes it clear that he treats people as self-organising, dynamic and emergent. He explained that he works with an incentive system. *'We have staff who are waiting for a call to provide work for them'* and when a shipment is scheduled to arrive he telephones these people. Phil prioritises his calls, choosing people according to how well they perform, their willingness to undertake hard physical labour, their attitudes and ways of relating to other crewmembers and the clients. A rate for unpacking the containers is offered to the workers, according to the content of the container, and this is set in (for example) $1000 lots. It is up to those working in each crew to determine their own processes and practices. In other words, the work of the individuals and crews is set within a space that has very little pre-existing structure and rules to it. The expectation is that those doing the unpacking will manage the ways by which this work is accomplished. The only guideline is that the systems the crews develop must be within industry guidelines (such as those of Occupational Health and Safety).

The incentive system means that the crews determine the efficiency of their processes and how quickly or slowly they complete the unpacking. The daily hours of employment are thus under the control of the workers themselves. Phil says that because many people are used to being told what to do, they need to be encouraged to think of ways of working that are more effective for health and safety or other reasons. All are thrilled to leave work by as early as around 1.00pm, knowing that the remainder of the day is theirs to do with as they please.

It is interesting that Phil sees the focus on broadening his communication, relational and motivational skills as essential to his role. Rather than directly managing and controlling the activities of the crews, he acts as facilitator and motivator, and believes that his role in this regard is to generate momentum. He concentrates on promoting *communicative connectedness* and coherence between himself as operations manager, the crewmembers and the overall aims of the company.

Phil notes that many of the people he works with aspire to the idea of 'one job for life' with KIA-Contractors – they are looking for full-time, permanent and secure employment. In his view this is not a realistic or useful aim. Rather, he advocates that people think in terms of opportunities for maintaining (at least) a basic standard of living, for learning new skills and for personal development. His management style is clearly an outworking of these views. For example, self-management of time, as Barry Jones (former Australian Minister for Science) points out, *is central to personal development, from infancy on* (2007:323), so having the crews set their own priorities and self-manage their time is facilitative of personal development.

Phil goes further, though, in advocating that the employees think of themselves not as mere 'labourers' but as 'business managers' of themselves: *'If I was in their position, I'd be keeping a portfolio in my mind about where else I could go if KIA-Contractors let me go. I'd be thinking about how to learn a range of skills so that I could constantly improve my lifestyle and employment opportunities.'* He also encourages people to accept the complexity of today's working environment, arguing that *'It is not such a bad thing. If you become rooted in a certain job, way of living and way of thinking then you're in for a big shock. Perturbations do come. Surely having some foreknowledge helps you cope better.'*

The *initial conditions* for the establishment of KIA-Contractors were that the company was set up by, and comprised of, Maori and Pacific Island indigenous people. As Phil points out, there is clearly a strong dependence on these *initial conditions*. Although over time people with other backgrounds have been employed, they have not stayed. The *attractor* for employment in the crews seems to be bound up with participation in the community, having a large amount of personal autonomy over work processes and practices and greater lifestyle opportunities.

As Phil concludes: *'We sell a lifestyle. Maoris and Pacific Islanders are the only ones who stay. Maybe it's related to tribalism and the competitiveness and nuances peculiar to us as a people. Sharing our food, working in our indigenous ways to bring fun into what is otherwise a pretty basic, routine and boring job.'*

4.5 *Identification of pattern and potentiality in fractal fragment (7) Australian Stuttering Research Centre*

In Chapter 1, I quoted Mark's reflection on the way the Australian Stuttering Research Centre operates. To recapitulate:

'We get things done by sheer creative driving excitement and people who can do it. In general we are devoid of any known management structure in the universe. We don't say things like "they're not problems, they're challenges". We don't have lines of authority; we don't do change management. It's organised chaos.'
Professor Mark Onslow, Australian Stuttering Research Centre

I liked his response because of the way it immediately threw out a challenge to me and because I wanted to write yet another book (this book) advocating certain preferred ways of seeing and doing in organisations.

The Australian Stuttering Research Centre exists as an independently funded centre within the University of Sydney. It is supported financially by various large and prestigious competitively gained research grants, totalling around $6-7 million. *'We do research. We know a great deal about very little. Our core business is producing and disseminating research on stuttering,'* Mark explained. He and his colleagues take part in a multitude of research projects, participate in conferences, work with speech pathologists and other professionals, and undertake community service with people who stutter.

In terms of the day-to-day work, Mark describes the Centre as largely being *'a centre without walls'*. He elaborated: *'There are only 3.6 full-time academic researchers permanently employed. All the rest are a floating population, people working on projects funded by grants. This includes a large number of research students and colleagues from other institutions around the world. One of our current projects, for example, consists of a consortium of people in seven different countries, representing eleven different institutions.'*

Mark exudes excitement about his work, saying that, *'We develop projects for fun. We work on projects funded by grants. We have an idea. We toss it around and decide who could do it. As the idea is developed, it's immediately apparent who the stakeholders might be. We'll send out an email to all those we think have something to contribute, asking, "Who wants to be in on this?" This is really a code for "who wants to do some work and get their name on a publication". The other way we work is when we have a grant in place and we ask one of our research assistants to manage a particular aspect of it.'* He attributes the success of the Centre to having people involved *'who have the talent and ability to work extraordinarily productively and creatively.'*

I was interested to find out about how the Centre maintained *communicative connectedness* with so many people working out of multiple locations and on a diverse range of projects. *'It's extraordinarily complicated,'* he agreed. *'We have 2-3 regular meetings each week, with phone and skype link-ups as necessary. And we have a small team of people working on the administrative side of things. We [Mark and the other permanently employed academics] work*

4. IDENTIFYING PATTERNS AND POTENTIALITY

with these people allocating tasks as appropriate. I manage 'Mantrack', an excel program that tracks the 50 or so manuscripts we have at any time in various stages of preparation. I have one of the administrative people assist me with this. For example, if a writer does not meet a deadline, she will send out an email noting this and saying 'That's fine, but your name will not be on the publication.' He went on, *'At the moment, we are concurrently running 45 clinical trials across 45 projects involving hundreds of participants. So it's important that we have someone coordinating who is working on what and interacting with who where.'*

On visiting the Centre and taking part in their meetings, I could feel enthusiasm and an excited busyness around me. Here were intelligent, thoughtful people engaging passionately in their quest to better understand the causes and effects of stuttering and how to most efficaciously offer support and ameliorative treatment for people who stutter.

You cannot run such an organisation without formal attention to structure unless, as is clearly the case for the Australian Stuttering Research Centre, a powerful *attractor* holds the organisation together. Here the *attractor* is passion for research into stuttering. The Centre draws people to it, existing as a force field of passionate inquirers. The excitement is infectious, as is the accompanying sense of engagement in a worthwhile project and working together with really talented and capable people. Why would you encumber that with rules, when the *attractor* is so strong?

In addition to working around a strong *attractor*, there are other factors affecting the successful operation of the Centre. The people involved have to be able to cope with its 'organised chaos'. They need to be skilled in working independently and able to accommodate the schedules and needs of others – the kind of people who can live with uncertainty and chaos. People who seek to control uncertainty, who like order and routine, are unlikely to find the Centre a good fit with their personality type and values. A self-selection process ensures that only those who do fit with the culture and work processes of the Centre continue to work there. As Mark says, *'Only a certain type of person will work in this chaotic environment. It suits conceptual people.'*

Strong *communicative connectedness* is critical. As Mark reflected: *'To make this kind of chaos work, you need to be a much more skilful communicator than in other systems where you have a chief executive officer and heads of departments. There, the only communication you need is "I'm the boss". But to hold this Centre together you've got to be able to communicate clearly, concisely and openly. You've got to be able to communicate inspiration and trust. You've got to create an airborne piece of magic.'*

Scale matters. An increase in scale brings with it the influence of other *attractors*. Associated fields start to attract. When more and more people are brought in, more possible *attractors* are brought to the field. Over time, this is usually seen as variation in the field. One of the ways that scale is dealt with by the Centre is through a small enduring team of 3.6 academics. However, in recent times, the complexity of running so many concurrent projects has necessitated employment of a growing number of administrative support staff. This represents variation in priority tasks. Now, for some people (those working in administration), there is a second 'core business', a second *attractor*, that of successfully managing the Centre.

Over the time that I have been interacting with the Centre, I have observed a repeated turnover in administrative staff. In my view, this is unfortunate. It places added pressure on the academic staff, requiring them to engage in the recruitment and selection processes, the settling in and socialisation of new administrative staff, as well as managing exiting processes for those leaving. In its present form, there are two separate groups of people working towards two different *attractors* and the challenge for the future success of the Centre, I suggest, is learning how to marry these two *attractors*.

4. IDENTIFYING PATTERNS AND POTENTIALITY

4.6 A very useful attractor set

In this section a tripartite *attractor* set is introduced. My colleagues and I have found this useful in identifying pattern and potentiality in a variety of organisational settings (see, for example, Woog and Dimitrov, 2004 and Levick, Woog and Knox, 2007).

Given the nature of human beings, you might think that the number of *attractors* that could be recognised in social systems would border on the infinite. In a sense you are right. However, we have found that it is possible to identify a surprisingly narrow range of just three powerful *attractors* around which social systems, large and small, formal and informal, transient and enduring, are organised. I think of these as underlying *attractors* of which other identified *attractors* are specific time and place related expressions. Taken together I imagine these three *attractors* – *identity*, *access to resources* and *will to power* – as a very useful, *universal human attractor set*. This is modelled in Figure 7.

> I imagine these three attractors – *identity*, *access to resources* and *will to power* – as a very useful, *universal human attractor set*.

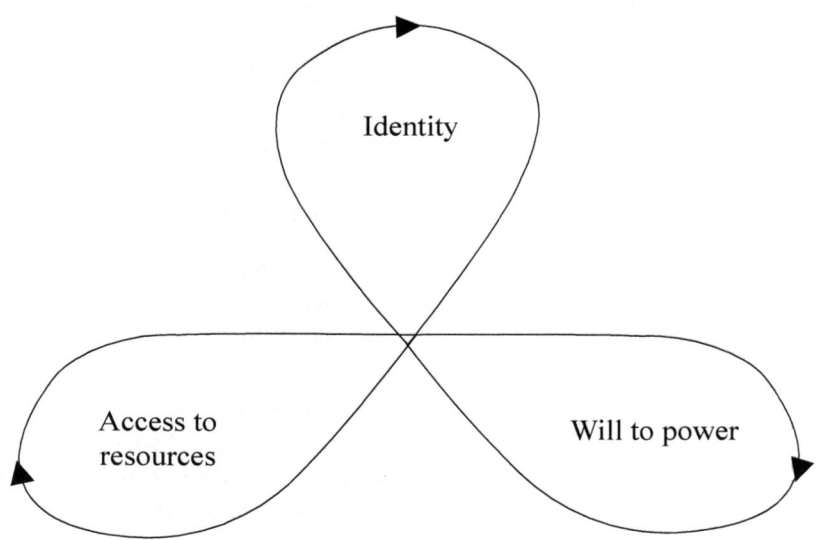

Figure 7
Universal Human Attractor Set

Each of these three *attractors* requires some elaboration. Although I could begin with any, I choose to start by describing the notion of *identity*. As a product of interactions between inherited characteristics, conscious action and self-reflection, *identity* can be described, in dynamic terms, as an ongoing process of construction with which we each engage. *Identity*, in other words, is self-organising, dynamic and emergent. Whether referring to an individual or a collective, *identity* is commonly understood as comprising three essential features (Melucci 1996):

1. The continuity of the subject (individual or group) over time and across changing circumstances. I remain myself even though I may change my employment situation, marital status, friends and musical tastes. Multi-national Pharmaceuticals remains Multi-national Pharmaceuticals even though it may have a new CEO, produce different drugs or even branch into new areas, enact different protocols, employ different people and so on.
2. The delimitation of this subject from others. I have a certain unity. I am not the same as others. I have my own thoughts and feelings. Multi-national Pharmaceuticals has its own unity. It is distinguishable from Pfizer, Fort Dodge and other pharmaceutical companies, its production partners, the various countries within which it operates and so on.
3. The ability to recognise and be recognised. I see myself as unique, a particular kind of person. We use differences from others in growing, defining and declaring our *identity*. We also use ideas of sameness for this purpose, recognising some others as 'one of us'. Other people recognise me as myself, as similar or different from them. I recognise other selves. Multi-national Pharmaceuticals is recognisable by its logo as well as by particular styles of production, packaging and advertising.

4. IDENTIFYING PATTERNS AND POTENTIALITY

Our identification of ourselves as certain kinds of people shapes interactions, behaviours and aspirations.

Identity is never a completed, taken-for-granted process. Our identification of ourselves as certain kinds of people shapes interactions, behaviours and aspirations. My behaviours will conform to my sense of 'this is who I am'. Some incentives will be more attractive than others, depending on the way I construct my *identity*. Perceived threats to *identity* result in strong reactions, both from individuals and collectives.

Fusion of individual and workplace identity is apparent when people talk of 'we', or 'our': we are all members of Multi-national Pharmaceuticals; we are the human resources staff; we are the New Zealand branch and so on. Entering and leaving organisations can be complicated because self-image and *identity* are implicated.

As an *attractor*, identity influences behaviours, dynamics and decisions.

As an *attractor*, *identity* influences behaviours, dynamics and decisions. Being aware of this and in endeavouring to identify pattern and potentiality, we can ask: Does the individual or collective (team, department, division, organisation, sector etc.) appear to be acting as if they see the continuity of their *identity* (individual or collective) as under threat in this situation? Or is it that the individual or collective is wishing to demonstrate their separation from others? Do they appear to be motivated by a need to assert their separateness? Does the individual or collective appear to be keen to declare the uniqueness of their *identity*? Are they asking others to recognise them in a particular way?

To maintain the integrity of our *identity* as well as our difference from others we require *access to resources*. Beyond the simple descriptors of food, shelter and companionship, people require access to quite particular resources. I may be vegetarian, someone who likes to eat organically, or only Kosher or Halal prepared foods. Or I may like to be seen with a Coca-Cola in my hand. To function as Multi-national Pharmaceuticals, the company requires access to a range of technologies, natural resources, energy, finances, chemists and other specialists and so forth. It also needs access to markets, storage facilities, means of transportation etc.

4. IDENTIFYING PATTERNS AND POTENTIALITY

To help understand pattern and potentiality, you should note the implications for *access to resources* for the various actors (individuals and collectives). Questions concerning what the desired resources are (information, knowledge, communicative partners, markets, time, energy and so on), as well as who is paying and who is benefiting, are pertinent.

The philosopher Friedrich Nietzsche proposed the *will to power* as a fundamental motivator in human behaviour (Nietzsche 1968). Nietzsche argued that there is no one truth, and that people attempt to have their views, beliefs, philosophies and interpretations of reality accepted by others. *Will to power* is the expression of the desire of people to exert themselves in their physical, social, spiritual, political and economic environment. We see the *will to power* manifested in all sorts of ways in personal and social life, in the drive to manage and control, to organise and overcome. Overt displays of the *will to power* are evidenced when management consultants and Chief Executive Officers argue over what is 'really going on' and what strategies are the best for ensuring future success.

In identifying pattern and potentiality, note attempts to colonise thinking and perception, to have others take the same view and interpret events in a particular manner. The *will to power* may also be seen in attempts to deny or facilitate *access to resources,* or to set up particular liaisons.

To show you how this universal *attractor* set can be used to inform understanding, I will use it as a basis for developing propositional analyses of two fractal fragments. In reading these examples, however, please bear in mind that they are based on a fairly limited engagement with the people and organisations concerned. If I were working with an organisation, I would introduce repeated cycles of reflective conversation with the participants to ensure that the analysis was true for them, as is evident when there is an 'Ah ha' response.

Consider fractal fragment (5). The *identity attractor* for Multi-national Pharmaceuticals is pre-eminence as a pharmaceutical company. This is seen through the company's desire to increase creativity so as to retain a market leadership position. The access to resources *attractor* implicates access to creative and organised people (for example, people able to meet necessary protocols as well as people able to create new products, new and better means of production, successful advertising campaigns, etc.), as well as access to ingredients, industry and government partners and so on. The *attractor will to power* is seen in the company's expressed desire to remain eminent and highly competitive. It is clear that each of these *attractors* drives behaviours and that taken together we can see what drives the organisation as a whole.

The *attractor* set can similarly be used to interrogate what motivates individual sections or employees. Take, for example, Jay and Bilal (fractal fragment (1) in Chapter 2). The *identity attractor* for Jay and Bilal can be seen as a coupling together of independence and responsibility. They enjoy setting their own hours, making their own appointments, arranging their own workspaces and so on. The resources they require access to are their company vehicles, Internet connectedness to all of the appropriate programs of Outreach Loans Bank and so on. The *will to power* relates to Jay and Bilal's capacity to undertake their work in their own ways and at their own rates. For example, we see this expressed as their desire to work with head office in particular ways.

4.7   *Complexity, self-organisation and ethical management*

A link can be made between the self-organising capacity of humans and ethical concerns. Drawing on philosophical discourse about characteristics essential to what it means to be a human being, I want to parse out elements of self-organisation as these pertain uniquely to people, and discuss implications for ethical management in organisational settings.

As stated in preceding chapters, complexity provides a framework for making sense of and working with complex phenomena. In so doing, complexity offers evocative ways of describing the functioning of people, both as individuals and as collectives. Complexity, as such, is not concerned with morals and ethics. But we humans are. We are inescapably ethical beings, concerned with what it means to live with a good conscience, about what it means, in particular circumstances, 'to do the right thing'.

Within western moral philosophy there have been long standing debates about whether there are special qualities that distinguish human beings from other animals. It has generally been agreed that indeed there are. From my perspective, it is possible to postulate four qualities essential to human beings (Kainz 1988, Kane 1994, Weston 1997). I see these qualities implicated in the unique self-organising capacities of humans. Understanding this provides insight into principles that can guide ethical management approaches, as well as insights into why people may react badly to certain circumstances. Appreciation of these qualities helps us manage in ways that will generate greater coherence rather than stressful and unproductive dynamics between those involved.

> Appreciation of these qualities [essential to human beings] helps us manage in ways that will generate greater coherence rather than stressful and unproductive dynamics between those involved.

The four essential qualities of human beings, through which our self-organisation capacities manifest themselves, are that we are:

1. self-determining
2. rational
3. self-conscious
4. socially conscious.

As *self-determining* beings we are internally driven, having the capacity to decide for ourselves what we feel and think and how we will behave. To behave ethically towards others means to respect them as self-driven and not to treat them as mere instruments for achieving our purposes.

> To behave ethically towards others means to respect them as self-driven and not to treat them as mere instruments for achieving our purposes.

4. IDENTIFYING PATTERNS AND POTENTIALITY

Understanding humans as *rational* underpins the variety of versions of 'The Golden Rule': '*Do unto others, as you would have them do unto you*'. This rule assumes that we can each make choices about what we do, and assumes that others are like us in their responses to things done to them. In this context, being rational means being able to extrapolate from particular instances to form general understandings and establish broad principles. It also means being consistent rather than self-contradictory, having the capacity to distinguish means from ends, and having the ability to moderate our impulses.

Being *self-conscious* means that we are aware of ourselves as individual beings. Philosophers as far back as Socrates, who lived 400 years before the Common Era, have exhorted people to learn about themselves; what drives them, what are their limits, and so on. Socrates went so far as to claim that *'the unexamined life is not worth living'*. Developing an understanding of yourself will enhance your ability to make a unique contribution to the world. It means you can develop greater empathy for others and make sense of situations with greater clarity because you will be better able to separate your own issues from your reading of situations.

As *socially conscious* beings, we are aware of others, and also aware that our ways of being and our ideas about the world both influence and are influenced by the social settings within which we exist.

In organisational settings, the ways that we interact with others and either manage or are managed by them really matters. Our self-consciousness, rationality and social consciousness are always implicated. In managing others, our ideas about who we are, what is fair or sensible, what we may expect from others, shapes what we do and say. Similarly, in being managed by others, our reaction to them is shaped by our ideas about who we are, what is fair or sensible or what we may expect from others. Individual and collective self-organisation, dynamism and emergence thus arise out of multiple exchanges between humans

> Developing an understanding of yourself will enhance your ability to make a unique contribution to the world... [to] develop greater empathy for others and make sense of situations with greater clarity...

> Our self-consciousness, rationality and social consciousness are always implicated. In managing others, our ideas about who we are, what is fair or sensible, what we may expect from others, shapes what we do and say.

as self-determining, rational, self-conscious, and socially conscious beings.

In endeavouring to identify pattern and potentiality, you can use awareness of these four qualities of humanness to help you analyse situational dynamics as well as predict future dynamics and emergence. This is what I did when I told the story, in Chapter 1, of my son and his blue hair. Fussing with his appearance represented my son's self-organisation as a self-determining, rational, self-conscious and socially conscious being. Allowing him to experiment meant that, in this regard, we were not at odds with each other and allowed the dynamics between us to be more coherent and facilitative of better *communicative connectedness*. Similarly, understanding these aspects of self-organisation assists us in how we work with others, particularly when we are in a leadership or managerial role.

> I suggest that ethical management practices are those that enhance and promote self-determination, rationality, self-consciousness and social-consciousness.

I now want to discuss implications for ethical management in organisational settings. I suggest that ethical management practices are those that enhance and promote self-determination, rationality, self-consciousness and social-consciousness. To this end, I propose an *ethical management check list*. I suggest that you ask yourself:

1. To what extent do my behaviours as manager protect and promote self-determination in others and myself? One way that self-determination can be compromised is through forcing people to take refuge in a role. When someone says things like 'I did it because I am the night duty manager', or 'because I am the accountant charged with cutting costs', they are depicting their decisions and actions as tied to a role, rather than based on their own decisions as self-determining individuals. When people do not feel safe to engage thoughtfully and fully, they may take refuge in their role.
2. To what extent do my behaviours as manager protect and promote rationality of others

and myself? One way that rationality is undermined is through the use of incentives, which are often promoted as an effective tool in getting things done in particular ways (faster, more economically, through making more sales and so on). Incentives serve to encourage people to act in particular ways, either because they are fearful of punishment or expect a reward. In both cases, the use of incentives undermines rational reflection because it causes us *to look to others for thoughts about what is best to pursue and even worthy of our efforts.* (Sanford 1994:27) The danger with this is that we slowly lose the ability to assess our own actions and their appropriateness, and to test and upgrade our own thinking (Sanford ibid).
3. To what extent do my behaviours as manager protect and promote the self-consciousness of others and myself? Any management style that requires blind allegiance to rules or which appeals to displays of loyalty are counter to fostering people's ability to behave in accordance with their own self-conscious and rational judgements.
4. To what extent do my behaviours as manager protect and promote the social consciousness of others and myself? Management that treats people as if they are working in a social vacuum, that does not recognise our need to relate to the world around us, serves to diminish our social consciousness.

Understanding that our behaviour as managers can serve to promote and protect or, conversely, undermine the four identified qualities of humanness, we are better informed about the consequences of our actions, the likely impacts on situational dynamics and the implications for future emergence. For example, if my managerial style leads people to take refuge in a role, to focus on working towards incentives, to depict blind allegiance and ignore sensitive social issues, then it should come as no surprise that when I ask for innovative and original solutions to problems there are no suggestions forthcoming. For my behaviour has served to undermine individuality and to foster compliance and unreflective, unaware ways of being. I am reminded of the account, in Steven Jay Gould's book *The Mismeasure of Man* (1981), of why slaves in America, at the end of a day of hard work, thoughtlessly trampled over the very plants they had planted. The 'scientific' argument put forward at the time was that the slaves were suffering from an illness called *dysesthesia*. Today, we would attribute this behaviour to the debasing influence of slavery, for here we see in exaggeration the effects of such violation of individual autonomy on the self-organising capacities of people.

We can act with awareness, understanding that if our style of management is not respectful of the personhood of those with whom we interact, we will generate responses and behaviours not conducive to the future sustainability and prosperity of the organisation. For if the self-organisation of people is muted or reactive to a style of interaction and management that does not promote the full potential of those involved, then both individuals and the whole organisation suffer. To foster the capacity to read pattern and potentiality we need people, as D. H. Lawrence puts it, *'in their wholeness wholly attending'*.

Further reading

Complexity and organisations

Kuhn, L. and Woog, R. (2007) 'From Complexity Concepts to Creative Applications', *World Futures: The Journal of General Evolution.* Vol 63, Nos 3-4, April – June, pp.176 – 193.

Kuhn, L., Woog, R. and Hodgson, M. (2003) 'Applying Complexity Principles to Enhance Organisational Knowledge Management', *Proceedings, Global Business and Technology Association Conference: Challenging the Frontiers in Global Business and Technology: Implementation of Changes in Values, Strategy and Policy, Budapest, Hungary,* July 8-1, pp. 754-7622.

Kuhn, L., Woog, R. and Knox, K. (2006) *Repositioning Young People in a Communicative Landscape: Research into the Design and Development of the Hebersham Aboriginal Youth Service*. University of Western Sydney. April 2006

Levick, D., Woog, R. and Knox, K. (2007) 'Trust and Goodwill as Attractors: Reflecting on a Complexity-informed Inquiry', *World Futures: The Journal of General Evolution.* Vol 63, Nos 3-4, April -June.pp.250 - 264.

Philosophically interesting

Gould, S. J. (1981) *The Mismeasure of Man*. New York: Norton.

Kainz, H. P. (1988) *Ethics in Context.* London: Macmillan Press.

Kane, R. (1994) *Through the Moral Maze*. London: North Castle Books.

Nietzsche, F. (1968) *Basic writings of Nietzsche.* W. Kaufmann, (trans). New York: Random House.

Weston, A. (1997) *A Practical Companion to Ethics.* Oxford: Oxford University Press.

5. ORGANISING AT THE EDGE OF CHAOS

5.1 Competencies commensurate with organising at the edge of chaos

Organising effectively at the *edge of chaos* requires attentiveness, a capacity to move from focus on detail in local circumstances to identification of pattern and potentiality more globally. Flexibility is needed in order to decide when to stick with identified 'core' business, mission statements or other such definers of perception and action, and when to intervene and trigger potential change in form, process and practice. Thus managers working within the complexity paradigm who seek to position their organisation near the *edge of chaos* (that region where potentiality is maximised), will need to be thoughtful about identifying competencies that are commensurate with this aim.

A complexity approach to making sense of organisational forms, processes and practices inevitably implicates ways of doing. Just as in Aristotle's time, taking slavery for granted meant there were certain work practices (tasks undertaken by slaves under the direction of masters), so viewing people and organisations as complex has implications for the ways by which organisational life is accomplished. Throughout the book I have included discussion of the practical implications of the complexity principles and metaphors introduced. In this section I want to emphasise these more, by offering suggestions for competencies commensurate with a complexity-based view, especially to those charged with various management responsibilities. I say 'especially' because, as shown throughout, in taking a complexity view of organisations, organisational manifestation is seen as less to do with powerful individuals, who manage and control, and more to do with the qualities of *communicative connectedness* between people as self-organising, dynamic and emergent beings. From a

> ... organisational manifestation is seen as less to do with powerful individuals, who manage and control, and more to do with the qualities of *communicative connectedness* between people... .

5. ORGANISING AT THE EDGE OF CHAOS

complexity perspective, everyone who is involved in the organisation contributes to its management.

With a scientific management approach, a strict hierarchy of responsibility is necessary. Certain competencies are required of managers charged with responsibility for work practices within this hierarchy. Managers need skills for accurately measuring efficiency of work practices, the ability to break down jobs into separate, measurable components and the capacity to reward and punish workers for their compliance or non-compliance. Those managed in this way need the capacity to do the work as directed and an ability to work compliantly under the overt mechanisms of strict control.

> From a complexity perspective, everyone who is involved in the organisation contributes to its management.

A complexity framework for getting things done, however, brings a need for quite different capabilities and skills that, rather than being tied to specific roles, are required of the organisation as a whole. It is more likely that these competencies will be distributed throughout the organisation, crossing functional and hierarchical boundaries.

5.2 What can an organisation do to enhance its opportunities in a complex world?

The following suggestions sketch possible approaches or actions (these may be interpreted as complexity-based competencies) for enhancing organisational opportunities in a complex world. I have tried to describe them in an open way, indicating applicability across multiple fractal levels (individual, group, section, department, sector and so on).

1. *Facilitate permissive approaches to getting things done.* Be supportive of innovative communication, relationship and community-developing activities. This will give functional groups greater freedom to work things (issues, alternative problem constructions or solutions etc.) through. The organisation has to be

flexible in regard to distributed functionality. Strong hierarchies only bring added tensions, as the boundaries they introduce and seek to protect become part of the dynamism of interaction between multiple self-organising entities. Recall fractal fragment (2) describing Anna's experience of working within the 'very hierarchical' National Counselling Service. Anna spent much time and energy actively self-organising to manage the limitations caused by the strong hierarchical structure of the organisation.

2. *Legitimate, and give time for, adaptive developmental activities.* To flourish, organisations have to be open to emergence. As demonstrated by Multi-national Pharmaceuticals in fractal fragment (5), creativity and developmental directions come from a broad range of sources, and the timeframe for these cannot always be mandated in advance. Casual and indiscriminate mingling and association enrich potentiality. Therefore, facilitate permissive approaches and legitimise the time allocated for adaptive developmental activities.

3. *Respect the small because the small is everything.* A complexity view of organisations illustrates that the small things of everyday life really matter because by this means societies are created, developed and maintained. How we speak to and treat one another, or the systems and rules guiding operations, shape individual consciousness as much as organisational emergence. Human perceptions, choices and actions arise from the dynamics of daily interactions between people. With large portions of our life spent in organisations, especially organisations as firms – collectives of employment – most daily interactions are within organisations. So the dynamics of the organisations, within which we are immersed and complicit, are critical in forming perceptions, choices and actions.

Sometimes small patterns reoccur. Sometimes small changes are responsible for major changes. Therefore, small matters.
4. *Promote democratic individuality.* As it is through people that organisations get things done, there is good reason to support individual freedom of development and thus promote maximal room for individual variation. Organisations need the involvement of thoughtful, fully engaged people. Given the purposive, goal-driven nature of organisations, how can maximal variability of individuals be supported within organisational settings? To simply advocate support for individual self-development is naive because individuals may hold different or even competing goals, and these may only tangentially mesh with the goals of the organisation. Democratic individuality gives individuals maximum room for 'play', (as in the movement of a pivot pin loosely positioned within its housing), for discernment and choice within boundaries. In an organisation such boundaries may more resemble a continuously constructed field of possibilities and limits. If a dance sequence is too prescriptive, jerky movement results. If the dance is to be beautiful, more freedom is necessary. One of the hardest things to do in support of democratic individuality is to relinquish individual ego, to admit that the organisation learns its way and emerges as an interrelating collective rather than through the guidance of a specific individual. Promoting democratic individuality means devolving responsibility and facilitating strong *communicative connectedness*.
5. *Take care over quality of interactions.* I have drawn attention to the importance of local relationships throughout this book and, hence, the quality of *communicative connectedness* to the overall emergence of the organisation. Non-censorious interaction (non-blaming and shaming, etc.), where expression of

maximal individual variation is protected, will mean more energised coherent dynamics of emergence. A wider variety of perceptions and perspectives will be available, thus enriching the variety of knowledge and information accessible to the organisation.

6. *Use mutual reconceptualisation to address (difficult) situations, rather than mutual negation.* Mutual reconceptualisation says 'Well here we are, what may we anticipate next?' rather than 'the situation is your/mine/their fault' or 'this is a really bad situation, we might not survive this'. Mutual reconceptualisation asks everyone involved to contribute to developing a new understanding and appreciation of the situation, based on a non-judgemental attitude. Engaging in mutual reconceptualisation addresses the potentiality associated with adaptive self-organisation. So, rather than viewing situations as right or wrong, it is accepting them for what they are – manifestations of adaptive self-organisation. It means accepting what manifests, rather than trying to stick with a pre-arranged agenda.

However, a host of prerequisites, such as honesty, the ability to express yourself, to trust and be trusted, underpin engagement in mutual reconceptualisation. For this to occur, an egalitarian permissive environment is required – and this takes us back to all of the above points. Mutual reconceptualisation does not flow from hierarchy but from self-organising forces within.

Recognise the varying capabilities that people have for fostering adaptive self-organising adjustments. It would be advantageous to have someone, who understands the process of what is involved in making adaptive self-organising adjustments, to act as facilitator of the process of mutual reconceptualisation. This person may be in an identified management or leadership position.

7. *Open discourse.* Open the discourse between people, and between mission and potentiality. With people, organisations and contexts being self-organising, dynamic and emergent there will be a permanent tension between the continuous metamorphosis, the redefinition of mission and purpose, and the need to stabilise boundaries. Too much focus on mission or purpose can be limiting, and may even render the organisation out of sync with its fitness landscape. By facilitating information from a broader range of people, and by opening up the breadth of topics to be addressed, the organisation will draw in information about cultural climates and expectations and thereby enhance its likelihood of achieving peaks within its fitness landscape.

8. *See in yourself the change you wish to achieve.* Recognise the difficulty and risk associated in acting in the ways suggested above, particularly because of the paradigmatic history of strong boundaries associated with delegated roles, accountability and productivity. Taking into account *sensitive dependence on initial conditions*, it should not be surprising that scientific management or rational bureaucratic approaches continue to influence organisational practices today. Similarly, there are echoes in scientific management and rational bureaucratic approaches that reach right back to the slave management practices of ancient Greek society.

You may not be able to completely separate yourself and your practices from such influences. Neither is this a requirement. What is suggested is that you engage in a process of becoming habitually thoughtful, of thinking about what you do and where the underlying logic comes from. You can ask yourself about the assumptions guiding your behaviours: What are my underlying beliefs about how best to get things done? Are they based on an

> What is suggested is that you engage in a process of becoming habitually thoughtful, thinking about what you do and where the underlying logic comes from.

interconnected and relational model or one of power and control? Understanding complexity principles and metaphors, how then should I enact my managerial responsibilities in the day-to-day ordinariness of organisation life? Rather than foolishly suggest you abandon or neglect inherited practices, I suggest you take a more creative approach and endeavour to find the complexity in them.

It can be tempting to dismiss many of the complexity principles and metaphors introduced in this book, by saying, 'but my organisation will not allow for that'. A way of responding to such a comment is to recognise that nobody is saying that you should act outside of your *initial conditions*. Every complex entity or system, from an individual person through to a nation state, finds itself, to some degree, within the bounds of its environment. Rather than set out to change its environment, complex entities self-organise. They adapt to work within their environment. Sometimes broad scale change comes from that. Sometimes the larger system develops its own adaptive, creative responses. For people, self-awareness is critical. Self-awareness is a different outcome and, even if circumstances prove quite limiting, the awareness of engagement and achievement is incredibly empowering to the individual. In this way, think of multiple outcomes, one of which may be that you have increased your awareness and understanding of your situation.

In the end you will evolve your own theoretical perspectives and your preferred styles of action and interaction. As an individual you have to take responsibility for yourself. Our self-organisation as self-determining, rational, self-conscious and socially conscious beings mandates this. So, in your ways of getting things done, be the change you wish to achieve.

REFERENCES

Ashby, W. (1962) *Principles of the self-organising system. Principles of self-organisation*: Transactions of the University of Illinois Symposium. H. Von Foerster and G. Zopf Jr. (eds.) London: Pergamon Press.

Bak, P. and Chen, K. (1991) 'Self-organised Criticality', *Scientific American.* January 1991.

Baets, W. (2006) *Complexity, learning and organisations.* London: Routledge.

Blake, W. (1994) *Selected Poems.* (Ed I. Hamilton). London: Bloomsbury Publishing.

Boje, D. M. (2001) *Narrative Methods for Organisational and Communications Research.* London: Sage.

Clegg, S., Kornberger, M. and Pitsis, T. (2005) *Managing and organisations.* London: Sage.

Complex adaptive systems (http://en.wikipedia.org/wiki/Complex_adaptive_system#cite_note-0)

Denning, S. (2000) *The Springboard: How Storytelling Ignites Action in Knowledge.* London: Butterworth-Heinemann.

Dillon, M. (2000) 'Poststructuralism, complexity and poetics', *Theory, Culture & Society* 17(5):1-26.

Fineman, S., Sims, D. and Gabriel, Y. (2005) *Organizing and organizations.* London: Sage

Friere, P. (1985) *The politics of education.* (Trans. Donaldo Macedo) Mass.: Bergin and Garvey.

Gleick, J. (1990) *Chaos: Making a New Science.* London: Cardinal.

Gould, R. (2007) 'Voices from the past, heard in the present, beckoning the future', Honours Thesis, University of Western Sydney, Australia.

Gould, S. J. (1981) *The Mismeasure of Man.* New York: Norton.

Grey, C. (2005) *A very short, fairly interesting and reasonably cheap book about studying organisations.* London: Sage.

Hodgson. G. (2000) 'The concept of emergence in social science: Its history and importance', *Emergence.* 2(4), 65-77.

Johnson, S. (2001) *Emergence.* Ringwood, Vic.: Penguin.

Jones, R. (1983) *Physics as Metaphor.* London: ABACUS

Jung, C. G. (1995) *Memories, Dreams, Reflections.* London: Fontana Press.

Kainz, H. P. (1988) *Ethics in Context.* London: Macmillan Press.

Kane, R. (1994) *Through the Moral Maze.* London: North Castle Books.

Kauffman, S. (1995) *At home in the universe: The search for the laws of self-organisation and complexity.* Oxford: Oxford University press.

Kelly, G. (1955) *The Psychology of Personal Constructs Vol 1 and 2.* New York: W. W. Norton and Company.

REFERENCES

Kuhn, L. and Woog, R. (2007) 'From complexity concepts to creative applications', *World Futures: The Journal of General Evolution.* Vol 63, Nos 3-4, April -June. pp.176 -193.

Kuhn, L., Woog, R. and Knox, K. (2006) 'Repositioning Young People in a Communicative Landscape: Research into the Design and Development of the Hebersham Aboriginal Youth Service', University of Western Sydney. April 2006.

Kuhn, L., Woog, R. and Hodgson, M. (2003) 'Applying complexity principles to enhance organisational knowledge management', *Proceedings, Global Business and Technology Association Conference: Challenging the Frontiers in Global Business and Technology: Implementation of Changes in Values, Strategies and Policy.* Budapest, Hungary, July 8-11, pp. 754-762.

Langton, C. (1986) 'Studying Artificial Life with Cellular Automata', *Physica* 22D: 120-49.

Levick, D., Woog, R. and Knox, K. (2007) 'Trust and Goodwill as Attractors: Reflecting on a Complexity-informed Inquiry', *World Futures: The Journal of General Evolution.* Vol 63, Nos 3-4, April – June.pp.250 – 264.

Lewin, R. (1999) *Complexity: Life at the edge of chaos.* Chicago: University of Chicago Press.

Lissack, M. (1999) 'Complexity: the science, its vocabulary, and its relation to organisations', *Emergence.* 1(1)110-126.

Lopate, P. (1995) *The Art of the personal Essay: An Anthology from the Classic Era to the Present.* New York: Anchor Book, Doubleday.

Mandelbrot, B. (1977) *The Fractal Geometry of Nature.* New York: Freeman.

Maturana, H. and Varela, F. (1987) *The Tree of Knowledge.* Boston, MA: Shambhala.

Mitleton-Kelly, E. (2006) 'Co-evolutionary integration: the co-creation of a new organisational form following a merger and acquisition', *Emergence: Complexity and Organisation* 8:2:36-47.

Mitleton-Kelly, E. (2006) 'A complexity approach to co-creating an innovative environment', *World Futures.* 62:223-239.

Nietzsche, F. (1968) *Basic writings of Nietzsche.* W. Kaufmann, (trans). New York: Random House.

Nonaka, I. (2004) *A dynamic theory of organisational knowledge creation.* Starkey, K., Tempest, S. and McKinlay, A. (ed's) *How Organisations Learn.* London: Thomson.

Packard, N. (1988) 'Adaptation Towards the Edge of Chaos', Technical Report, Center for Complex Systems research, University of Illinois, CCSR-88-5.

Rilke, R. M. (2004) *Letters to a Young Poet.* (Trans. M. D. Herter Norton) London: W. W. Norton and Company.

Robbins, S. and Barnwell, N. (2002) *Organisation Theory: Concepts and cases.* Frenchs Forest: Prentice Hall, Pearson Education Australia.

REFERENCES

Robinson, J. A. (1981) 'Personal Narratives Reconsidered', *Journal of American Folklore*, 94:58-85.

Rorty, R. (1998) *Truth and Progress, Philosophical Papers Vol 3*. Cambridge: Cambridge University Press.

Russell, B. 1995. *History of western philosophy*. New York: Routledge.

Sagar, K. (1972) *D. H. Lawrence Selected Poems*. Middlesex: Penguin Books.

Shaw, P. (2002 *Changing Conversations in Organisations*. London: Routledge.

Stacey, R. D., Griffin, D. and Shaw, P. (2000) *Complexity and Management*. London: Routledge.

Taylor, F. 1967. *Principles of scientific management*. New York: Harper.

Tutu, D. (1999) *No Future Without Forgiveness*. London: Rider.

Waldrop, M. 1992. *Complexity*. New York: Simon and Schuster.

Wenger, E. (2004) 'Communities of Practice and Social Learning Systems', Starkey, K., Tempest, S. and McKinlay, A. (ed's) *How Organisations Learn*. London: Thomson.

Weick, K.. (1995) *Sensemaking in Organisations*. London: Sage.

Weston, A. (1997) *A Practical Companion to Ethics*. Oxford: Oxford University Press.

Wilkinson, M. (Environmental Editor) (2008) 'Cold Rush for Arctic's Energy Riches', *The Sydney Morning Herald*, August 4.

Winterson, J. (2005) *Weight*. Melbourne: The text Publishing Company.

Wittgenstein, L. (1988) *Tractatus Logico-Philosophicus*. Trans. Pears, D. F. and McGuiness, B.F. London: Routledge and Humanities Press International.

Wolfram, S. 2002. *A New Kind of Science*. Champaign, IL: Wolfram Media.

Woog, R. (2004) The Knowing of Knowledge. Australian National Training Authority (2004) Working and Learning in Vocational Education and Training in the Knowledge Era. Available at http://www.flexiblelearning.net.au/projects/resources/PDFutureF.doc

Vickers, G. (1984) *Human Systems are Different*. London: Harper and Row.

Vygotsky, L. (1978) *Mind in Society: The Development of Higher Psychological Processes*. Cambridge: Harvard University Press.

About the Author

I have always been interested in and puzzled by the lived human condition. In meandering along the paths of an eclectic career, I have explored various aspects of human development. As a teacher, in education and learning, as a musician, in aesthetic appreciation, and as a thinker, I have sought to reflect about the cause and reason of things; hence my abiding interest in philosophy. At various times I have pursued one or other aspect of my interests through applied practice and research inquiry. My hopes are for a tolerant, democratic and egalitarian society. I want people to be aware of how they are structured and categorised by social and cultural dictates, ideologies and the declarations of those who think they have a monopoly on what is right and should be known. I am passionate about protecting and promoting flexibility and freedom of mind and soul along with a capacity for trust, wonder and hope.

I am presently employed as a Senior Lecturer in the College of Business at the University of Western Sydney, Australia. For 14 years prior to this I was positioned in the Social Ecology Centre, an innovative post-graduate-oriented transdisciplinary Centre that brought an integral or holistic perspective on the self, nature and society. I hold degrees in music, education, environmental science and philosophy, with my doctoral work focussing on the nature of epistemology and belief. Over the past 13 years I have been active in bringing complexity habits of thought to philosophical and social inquiry and in developing complexity informed ethnographic research approaches. I have authored more than 40 book chapters and published papers, and led more than 30 research projects. Most recently I led a complexity-informed research project into the needs of indigenous tertiary education students. In 2007 I was invited to be the Guest Editor for a special double issue of the prestigious journal, *World Futures: The Journal of General Evolution*, that was dedicated to showcasing the work of UWS academics in bringing complexity-informed approaches to social inquiry.

Testimonials

Lesley Kuhn has written a thoughtful, innovative and above all practical book about the implications and applications of complexity science for management. Written in a refreshingly engaging style, Kuhn's book manages to pack a lot of useful information in a relatively small book. In a field that has mostly been dominated by the revolutionary nature of the science with less emphasis on real-life applications, Kuhn has managed to provide the reader with a solid grasp of the science and a useful way of thinking about what it all means on Monday morning. *Adventures in Complexity. For organisations near the Edge of Chaos* is not only a major new contribution to the literature on management and complexity, but to the management literature as a whole.
Alfonso Montuori, Professor & Department Chair, Transformative Studies, California Institute of Integral Studies

Lesley Kuhn's new book, *Adventures in Complexity. For Organisations near the Edge of Chaos* provides a welcome link between the complexity science perspective and actual opportunities for action in organizations. Dr. Kuhn's combination of theory, narratives from the field, and suggestions for practice makes Adventures in Complexity a readable resource for both experienced leaders and students of leadership. Because of Dr. Kuhn's deep understanding of complexity and organizations, she is able to take material that others find daunting, and without sacrificing any depth, make it accessible to those who want to understand and apply the potential at the edge of chaos.
Deborah P. Bloch, Professor Emerita, University of San Francisco

In this smart little book – at times playful as well as thoughtful throughout – Lesley Kuhn gives impressive substance to the age-old claim that there is nothing as practical as a good theory. In her case, the theory is that which she refers to as the complexity sciences: The practices that are of concern to her are those that focus on the responsible and sustainable developments of organisations, which, with all of their peoples as components of them, characteristically exist, as she claims that they do, 'at the edge of chaos'. The mysteries of fractals and attractors, of potentialities and emergence, and of perspectives, narratives, discourse and metaphors for making sense of them all, are all engaging aspects of this very personal account of adventures in the complexity sciences as they relate to changing and change in organisations.
Richard Bawden, Adjunct Professor, Michigan State University
Professor Emeritus University of Western Sydney
Fellow and Director, Systemic Development Institute, Richmond, NSW

What I liked about Kuhn's approach from the beginning is the way she frames her object to be complex and inclusive. It is 'the life of organisations', not the more common 'organisation studies' nor the even more common 'management'. This deceptively simple, liberating decision shows her deft touch and accessible style. It also allows her to go beyond complexity theory and its well-meaning champions, and bring it back to life in both senses.
Bob Hodge, Professor of Humanities in the Centre for Cultural Research, University of Western Sydney

Kuhn's book brings a missing voice to the theme of organisations and complexity: the words and problems of ordinary people. Instead of being seduced but not transformed by complexity as is the case with many other management works, she convinces us to embrace complexity ways of thinking, talking about organisations to show how people's understanding of problems and solutions embraces non-linear forms of management.
Gabriela Coronado, Senior Lecturer in Organisation Studies, University of Western Sydney

www.ingramcontent.com/pod-product-compliance
Ingram Content Group UK Ltd.
Pitfield, Milton Keynes, MK11 3LW, UK
UKHW050215140126
466915UK00008B/108